A TradeQuillo Book

The Funded Edge

Futures, risk, and the quiet discipline
that gets you funded and keeps you there

James Mincy

TradeQuillo Press

First edition, 2026.
tradequillo@substack.com

Disclaimer
This book is for educational purposes only. Nothing in it constitutes financial, investment, tax, or trading advice. Trading futures and other leveraged instruments carries a substantial risk of loss and is not suitable for every investor. Because these instruments are leveraged, you can lose more than your initial deposit. Past performance is not indicative of future results. The characters and examples in this book are illustrative and do not represent real trading results or any specific person. Consult a qualified professional before making financial decisions.

Trademarks
All third-party trademarks, including E-mini, Micro E-mini, and Globex (CME Group Inc.) and VIX (Cboe), and all other exchange, index, platform, product, and company names mentioned in this book, are the property of their respective owners. They are used for identification purposes only, and their use does not imply endorsement, sponsorship, or affiliation.

Independence
This book is an independent publication. It is not affiliated with, sponsored by, or endorsed by any proprietary trading firm, exchange, broker, or trading platform, including any firm operating under a Funded Edge or similar name. The author does not endorse any particular firm.

Prices and figures
All prices, margin figures, and notional values in this book are illustrative snapshots, chosen for arithmetic clarity. Contract specifications, margin requirements, and market levels change constantly; always confirm current figures with the exchange and your broker before trading.

THE FUNDED EDGE

Foreword

There is an edge everyone is selling, and almost nobody has.

It is loud. It arrives in a Discord server with two thousand members, in a signal that pings your phone at 9:31, in an indicator with a Greek name and a color for every mood. It is sold by men standing in front of cars they rented for the afternoon. You have probably bought a version of it. Most traders have. It is the most expensive thing in this business, because it costs you money and it does not work.

This book is about the other kind of edge—the quiet one.

The quiet edge is the discipline, repeated, that is still solvent on Friday. It is the trader who is patient with risk, religious about stops, and humble about size, for long enough that a small advantage has time to compound. It is not a secret. You could walk right past it on a shelf. And it is the only edge that has ever actually funded a trader, because it is the only one that survives the part nobody posts about: the drawdown, the cold streak, the morning the account is red and the screen is quietly asking you to do something stupid.

I am going to attach a specific word to that edge, because it is the word this generation of traders is chasing, and they are right to chase it. Funded.

Here is what funded means, if the word is new to you. A proprietary trading firm hands you a much larger account than you could fund yourself. You trade it to a fixed set of rules. If you pass, you keep a share of what you make on the firm's capital. It is the most democratic thing to happen to trading in a decade, and futures are where it lives, because futures never had the rule that used to lock small accounts out. The on-ramp is wide open.

It is also a trap for the undisciplined, and the trap is the whole reason for this book. The evaluation that stands between you and a funded account is not really a test of whether you can find a trade. It is a test of whether you can hold your risk under control on someone else's clock, with money that is not yours, when it costs you something to do it. Most people fail that test. The honest estimates are blunt, and the firms mostly keep their precise numbers to themselves, which tells you something too. Something like one in seven passes a challenge. About one in fourteen ever reaches a payout. The other thirteen pay the fee, break a rule, and walk away, and almost none of them walk away because the strategy was wrong. They walk away because the person running it was not ready.

So here is the promise of the title, and of the whole book. The funded edge is the quiet one. The discipline that passes the evaluation is the same discipline that keeps the account after the first payout, which is the harder fight and the one nobody trains you for. Pass it, and keep it. That is the edge. It is unglamorous, it is repeatable, and it is yours to build.

You are going to build it next to two people.

The first is Marcus. Marcus is thirty-four, with a spare bedroom, two monitors he overpaid for, and a cousin in Austin who made four thousand dollars trading crude last week and will not stop talking about it. Marcus is the everyman, which is to say he is you on your first day, a little too hungry, certain the problem is finding the right setup. Over these chapters he learns the lesson that has to come first, the one the cousin never mentions, which is how not to die.

The second is Dani. Dani is further along. She has a method she half-trusts and the discipline to follow it most of the time. What she does not have, yet, is a funded account she can hold onto. She keeps buying evaluations and keeps failing them in the same few ways, never on the chart, always on herself: the loss she tried to win back, the setup she forced because the clock was running, the cushion she could not stop fiddling with until it was gone. She will meet, and name, all six of the traps this book is built around: the target trap, the give-back, the revenge trap, the mismatch, the hero day, and house money, and by the end she will own the countermove to each. Dani is the reader chasing the funded dream, and her fight is the one the title is named for. You will watch her pass, and then you will watch her face the part that is actually harder.

The third voice is Sal, and Sal does not fail at things, because he is sixty-one and came up in the Chicago pits before the screens ate them. Sal is the quiet edge already paid off: a man who forms a small precise hypothesis, sizes it so that being wrong costs him under one percent, places it, and then goes for a walk with his two bad knees and his dog. He does not hand Marcus and Dani answers. He builds the conditions that change what they do. Pay attention to Sal. He is what the other two are trying to become.

One more thing, said plainly, because honesty is most of what separates this book from the men with the rented cars. This book will make you literate in the market and keep you alive in it. It teaches futures from the ground up: what they are, who is on the other side of your trade, how the plumbing works, what risk really means when you can lose more than you put in, and how the evaluation is built so you can stop failing it for reasons that have nothing to do with the chart. What it cannot do, in sixteen chapters, is the deep work of rebuilding the mind that knows the rule and breaks it anyway, because in the moment a loss feels avoidable and you want it to be. That work has its own book. It is called Trade Calm, and by the time you finish this one, you will know exactly why you need it. Where the door is, I will point to it. I am not going to pretend this book is the whole house.

The loud edge is for sale on every timeline you scroll. The funded edge is not for sale at all. You have to build it, quietly, and once you have, it is the only thing in this business that is truly yours.

Let us begin.

CHAPTER 1

The Marathon, the Sprint, and the Bookies in Between

Marcus decided on a Sunday night, which is when most bad ideas and a few good ones get made.

He was thirty-four, he had a job he did not hate but did not love, a savings account earning almost nothing while a bank somewhere earned plenty on it, and a cousin in Austin who would not stop talking about the four thousand dollars he had made trading crude oil the week before. Marcus had a spare bedroom, two monitors he was about to overpay for, and a feeling, sitting just under his ribs, that he was tired of being on the wrong end of other people's money. So he opened a brokerage account, funded it, and decided he was going to learn to trade futures.

We are going to follow Marcus through this entire book, because the mistakes he is about to make are the mistakes the market has been collecting from beginners for two hundred years, and because watching someone make them is cheaper than making them yourself. Hold onto him. By the last chapter, he is a different trader. By the next chapter he is still the one who thinks his cousin found something the rest of us missed.

But before Marcus places a single trade, he needs to understand a thing that almost nobody explains to him, and that the cousin in Austin does not know he does not know. He is about to confuse two completely different jobs.

There is a useful lie that gets told to beginners: that trading and investing are the same activity performed at different speeds. Like walking and jogging, the lie says, like driving fifty-five versus driving seventy-five.

This is wrong in a way that matters.

Trading and investing are not the same activity at different speeds. They are different activities entirely, performed by different kinds of people, using different muscles, requiring different temperaments, and rewarding different virtues. Confusing them is the first mistake most aspiring traders make, and it costs them, sometimes literally, everything.

Let me show you what I mean.

The Investor

Picture a woman named Margaret. Margaret is fifty-three, lives in Pittsburgh, and works as a healthcare administrator. Twenty-six years ago she opened a retirement account, set up an automatic transfer of $300 a month, and bought a low-cost index fund. Then she did the single most lucrative thing a human being can do in financial markets: nothing.

She did not log in to check her balance. She did not panic in 2008 when the news anchors put on their grimmest neckties. She did not panic in 2020 when the world briefly ended. She did not call her brother-in-law, who has Opinions, and she did not move her money into gold because somebody on the radio said the dollar was about to collapse. The dollar, it should be noted, has been about to collapse for roughly seventy-five years. It has not yet collapsed. Somewhere, a man with a basement full of canned beans is very disappointed.

Margaret kept buying. She bought when prices were high. She bought when prices were low. She bought when she felt great about the world and when she felt terrible about it. Her account now holds a sum she does not quite believe is real. She is, by any reasonable definition, an investor.

Margaret made money by being patient with time.

The Veteran

Now picture a man named Sal.

Sal is sixty-one. He came up in the trading pits of Chicago in the years when a trade was a man shouting at another man across a wooden octagon, and he has the gravel voice and the two bad knees to prove it. When the pits died, and the screens ate them, Sal did what the good ones did. He adapted. Now he trades from a quiet room with three monitors and a coffee that he, unlike everyone else in this book, actually drinks while it is hot.

This particular morning it is 8:17, and in thirteen minutes the Bureau of Labor Statistics will release the monthly jobs report. Sal has read the consensus estimate. He has noted a level on the E-mini S&P 500 chart where he believes serious buyers are waiting. He has decided that if the number comes in soft, he will short the contract on the spike, with a target, and a stop, and a position size calibrated so that if he is dead wrong he loses well under one percent of his account. Then he does the part Marcus will not understand for another two hundred pages. He sits still. He does not lean forward. He has placed the trade in his mind, and the only thing left is to let the market either come to his level or not.

The number prints softly. The market shudders, gaps down through his level, hesitates, continues. Sal's order fills. Forty-seven minutes later he has covered, locked the profit, closed the platform, and gone for a walk with his knees and his dog.

Sal is a trader.

Sal made money by being precise about the present moment, and by having done it ten thousand times.

The One Chasing the Account

There is a third person in this book, and she is the reason for its title.

Dani is twenty-nine. She is not confused about the difference between Margaret and Sal. She knows she wants to be Sal, and she has put in more work than most people ever will: a method she has tested, a journal she actually keeps, the discipline to follow her rules on an ordinary Tuesday. What Dani does not have is enough money. Her own account is small, too small to make the time she pours into this worth it, and she knows it.

So Dani did what tens of thousands of capable, undercapitalized traders are doing right now. She went looking for someone else's money. She paid a proprietary trading firm a fee for an evaluation, a test: trade a simulated account their size, to their rules, hit a profit target without breaking a loss limit, and they will fund you for real and let you keep most of what you make. It is a genuinely good deal, and it is the most realistic path a small trader has to size that matters.

Dani has bought four evaluations. She has failed all four. Not one of them on her method. She failed the first when a loss she was sure would come back did not, and she sat in it past her stop. She failed the second when she shorted into a wall on the order book that turned out to be a mirage, and the slippage cost her three times what she had planned. She failed the third on a cluster of impatient counter-trend trades that each looked urgent and together bled her past the line by lunch. She failed the fourth while she was winning, giving back a cushion she could not stop fiddling with until it was gone. Every time, the strategy was fine. Every time, the person running it was not.

Dani's fight is the one this book is named for, because passing that evaluation, and then the harder part, keeping the funded account once she has it, is not a strategy problem. It is the quiet edge, tested under the brightest possible lights. We will come back to her often. By the end, she is funded, and still funded, which are two different achievements, and the second is the rare one.

The Difference, and Why It Matters to You

You can see, I hope, that Margaret and Sal are not doing the same job. Margaret's edge is time. She is renting growth from the global economy over a horizon of decades, and her primary skill is the willingness to sit still while other people lose their minds. Sal's edge is timing. He is renting volatility from the market over a horizon of minutes, and his primary skill is the ability to define a small, precise hypothesis about what is about to happen and to risk a controlled amount of money on it without his pulse changing. Dani has Sal's edge in everything but scale and nerve, and she is buying the scale and building the nerve at the same time, which is hard.

If Margaret tried to be Sal, she would be wiped out in a month. If Sal tried to be Margaret, he would die of boredom in a week.

Neither approach is morally superior. Neither is more real. Both can compound a small amount of money into a large one. But they are not interchangeable, and the great mistake of the beginner, the mistake Marcus is about to make, is to wander into a brokerage account, open a futures position because a cousin made $4,000 last week, and then try to behave like Margaret. Hold through the drawdown. Believe in the long-term thesis. Skip the stop, because he is confident. And then discover, in the way that men in movies discover the floor of an elevator shaft is unexpectedly close, that leverage does not care about his thesis.

This book is about being Sal, and about getting Dani funded. Before we can do either, we need to understand why futures trading is its own particular animal, and why so many people walk into it convinced it is a tame one.

What Makes Futures Different

A futures contract is, at its core, a remarkably simple promise. I will buy something from you, or sell something to you, at a price we agree on today, on a date in the future. That is the whole instrument. A farmer who promises in May to sell his October corn for $4.85 a bushel has entered a futures contract. A bakery that promises in May to buy that same corn at that same price has entered the other side of it. Each has taken a future uncertainty, what will corn cost in October, and converted it into a present-day certainty.

That is what futures were invented for. They are insurance for people who make and use real things, and they have been quietly doing that job for two centuries.

Then something happened. Once the contracts existed, and once they were standardized and traded on exchanges, a second group of people noticed you did not have to be a farmer or a baker to use them. You could buy the contract. You thought the price would go up, sell it because you thought it would go down, and never go near an actual bushel of corn. You could do this with crude oil, gold, the S&P 500, the ten-year Treasury note, the euro, the yen, soybeans, natural gas, lean hogs, and the cost of orange juice. Welcome to your new hobby.

A futures contract has four properties that, taken together, make it unlike anything else in finance. Know them by heart.

One: leverage that would make a banker blush. Buy a share of stock, and you put up the full price of the share. Buy a futures contract, and you put up a small fraction of its value, often three to ten percent, as a good-faith deposit called margin. The contract behaves as though you owned the whole thing. A standard E-mini S&P 500 contract represents roughly a quarter million dollars of exposure. To trade one, you might post around $13,000. If the index moves one percent in your favor, you make about $2,500, a large return on your posted capital. If it moves one percent against you, you lose about $2,500, and your broker will ring you, with no particular ceremony, asking for more. This is the cliff. It is closer than it looks.

Two: a two-way street. In a futures market, short is not a clever maneuver requiring special permission. It is exactly as easy as long. You can decide wheat is going to fall and sell a wheat contract you do not own with the same single click you would use to buy one. This is enormously useful, since markets fall faster than they rise, and the trader who can only profit going up spends a third of his career watching from the sidelines. It is also where beginners get tangled, because being short feels different from being long even when the math is symmetric.

Three: markets that essentially never close. U.S. stock markets are open six and a half hours a day, five days a week. The futures markets that matter, the S&P, the bonds, the energies, the metals, the currencies, run close to twenty-three hours a day. There is a brief, polite pause in the late afternoon for the system to breathe. Then it goes again. This sounds glamorous until the first time you wake at 3 a.m. to a notification that something happened in Tokyo and your position is no longer the position you went to bed with.

Four: standardization, liquidity, and depth that are frankly absurd. Every E-mini S&P contract is identical to every other. Enormous notional value changes hands every day. The bid-ask spread on the most liquid contracts is often a single tick, pennies of slippage on a quarter million dollars of exposure. There is essentially never a moment you cannot enter or exit a major contract. This is a feature, not a bug. It is what makes precise risk management possible. It is also what makes the markets unforgiving. When everyone can act instantly, they do.

Take those four properties, put them in a blender, and you get an instrument that can turn a small account into a meaningful one, and also, on a Wednesday morning, turn a meaningful one into a phone call to your spouse you would prefer not to make.

Why You Are Probably Here

Most people who buy a book like this are here for one of a few reasons.

The first is that they have some money, usually less than they pretend and more than they can afford to lose, and they have watched that money sit in a savings account earning almost nothing while a banker somewhere uses it to buy a boat. They are tired of being on the wrong end of that arrangement. Fair enough. This is Marcus.

The second is that they have a job they do not love, a commute they hate, and a fantasy in which trading replaces the job. The fantasy involves a laptop on a beach. It is a beautiful fantasy, and we will talk about it honestly in Chapter 16, the chapter where I try to talk you out of it for the right reasons and into it for the right ones.

The third is the one that has grown the fastest, and it is Dani's. They do not have enough capital of their own, and they have realized that a proprietary firm will rent them size if they can prove they deserve it. They are chasing a funded account. This is the largest new wave of traders in years, and futures are where it is happening, because futures never carried the rule that once forced small stock traders to keep twenty-five thousand dollars on hand to day-trade freely. That rule was finally scrapped in 2026, though some brokers are still phasing the change in. The on-ramp is as open as it has ever been, and it is crowded with capable, undercapitalized people who are about to learn that getting the account is the easy half.

The fourth is that something happened. They inherited money, or sold a business, or a parent died, or they reached a stage of life where they realized nobody is coming to manage their financial future for them. They decided, late or early, to become a more capable steward of capital than they are today. This is, in my experience, the best reason. People who arrive this way tend to last.

Whichever you are, the prerequisite is the same. You have to understand what you are actually doing. Not the trick. Not the system. Not the hot setup the cousin uses. The thing itself. What a market is. Who is on the other side of your trade. Why prices move. What risk really means when you can lose more than you put in. How to think about reward when leverage warps the math. And if you are Dani, how the evaluation that guards the funded account is built, and why it fails almost everyone for reasons that have nothing to do with the chart.

That is what this book is for. It will take sixteen chapters, and we are going to do it carefully, because the alternative, doing it carelessly, is what funds the salesman's rented Lamborghini.

A Word on the Word "Edge"

You are going to hear one word, over and over, from every trader and every book and every loud account online. Edge. Everyone claims one. Almost nobody can define it.

We will spend a full chapter on it later, because it is the hinge the whole enterprise turns on. For now, plant one sentence and let it sit. An edge is not a secret. It is a small, repeatable reason that the math of your trading comes out positive over a large number of attempts. That is all it is, and it is the rarest thing in this business, and most of what gets sold as an edge is a chart with three colored lines on it.

The kind of edge this book is built around is quieter still, because it is not a setup at all. It is the willingness to be patient with risk, religious about stops, and humble about size, repeated until a small advantage compounds, and held steady through the drawdown that breaks everyone else. That is the funded edge, the one in the title, and it is the only edge that ever actually passes an evaluation and keeps the account behind it. Sal has it. Dani is building it. The cousin in Austin has a winning week and a story. They are not the same thing, and the difference is most of the distance Marcus has to travel.

What We Are Doing in This Book

A quick map before we go.

In the chapters ahead, we build, piece by piece, the same skill set that gets traders funded and keeps them that way. We do it without jargon for its own sake, without the false certainty of the salesman, and without the airless complexity of the professor. We move through the fundamentals (Chapters 1 to 5), the analytical toolkit (Chapters 6 to 8), the strategies, the risk creed, and execution (Chapters 9 to 13), and finally, because this is the part nobody tells you matters most, the psychology and the long game of a trader who would like to be still trading, and still be funded, in ten years (Chapters 14 to 16). Dani's evaluation runs underneath the whole second half, because the rules she is fighting are the cleanest test there is of everything this book teaches.

That last part deserves a flag now, because it is where most traders actually fail, and where this book ends rather than begins. This is a field guide. It will make you literate in the market, competent with the instrument, honest about risk, and ready to walk into an evaluation knowing where its traps are. What it cannot do, in sixteen chapters, is the deep work of rebuilding the mind that operates under fire, the part of you that knows the rule and breaks it anyway because a loss feels avoidable in the moment. That work has its own book. It is called Trade Calm, and by the time you finish this one, you will know exactly why you need it. For now, know the door is there.

You will not, by the end, have a system. You will have something more valuable. A framework. A way of thinking. A vocabulary for diagnosing your own performance. A set of principles that work in oil and in bonds and in the S&P and in whatever new contract the exchange invents next year, and inside any firm's evaluation no matter how the rules are dressed.

You will also, I hope, have lost a certain kind of innocence, the kind that lets a person believe trading is easy, and gained in its place a sturdier kind of confidence. The confidence of someone who knows precisely how hard the thing is, has chosen to do it anyway, and has prepared accordingly.

So that is the plan. Let us begin with the simplest possible question, and one of the most consequential. The one Marcus has not thought to ask, because the cousin never mentioned it.

Who, exactly, is on the other side of your trade?

That is Chapter 2.

CHAPTER 1, KEY IDEAS

- **Trading and investing are different jobs, not different speeds of the same job.** The investor rents time from the global economy. The trader rents timing from the market. Confusing the two is the first expensive mistake, and it is the one Marcus is walking into.
- **A futures contract is a standardized promise** to buy or sell something at a set price on a set date. It was invented as insurance for businesses, then inevitably colonized by speculators.
- **Four properties make futures unique:** enormous leverage, symmetric long and short access, near-24-hour markets, and extreme standardization and liquidity. Together they create both unusual opportunity and unusual danger.
- **The funded path is the new front door.** A proprietary firm will rent you size if you can pass an evaluation. Getting the account is the easy half. Keeping it is the funded edge, and it is Dani's whole arc.
- **An edge is a small, repeatable reason your math comes out positive over many attempts.** The funded edge is quieter than any setup: patience with risk, stops honored, size kept humble, held through the drawdown. It is not a secret; it is rare, and a winning week is not one.
- **The number one job of a new futures trader is not to make money.** It is to have an account in twelve months still. Everything in this book is built around that.
- **The market will be literate in you long before you are literate in it.** This book closes the gap on the instrument and the evaluation. The mind that operates them is the work of Trade Calm.

CHAPTER 2

The Other Side of the Trade

Marcus placed his first trade on a Tuesday. He bought one E-mini S&P contract because the chart, to his eye, was going up, and for a few minutes it did, and he felt the specific electric pleasure of being right with money on the line. Then it stopped going up. Then it went down. He closed it for a small loss, annoyed, and asked himself a question he had genuinely never considered in his life.

When he bought that contract, who sold it to him? And why?

He did not have an answer. Most beginners never even reach the question. This chapter is the answer, and it is one of the most useful things in the book, because the stranger on the other side of your trade is never random, and learning to recognize the kinds of strangers who show up is worth more than any indicator you will ever buy.

Every time you click buy, a stranger somewhere clicks sell. Every time you click sell, a stranger clicks buy. That is the entire mechanism, and there is no exception to it. A market is, at its most reductive, an enormous matchmaking service for people who disagree.

So. Who is the stranger?

The stranger has a job. The stranger has a reason for being on the other side of your trade. That reason might be brilliant, or desperate, or automated, or regulatory, or a hedge against a completely different position, or it might be a 24-year-old in Florida who saw a video. You cannot know, in any single trade, which one it is. But over thousands of trades you can learn to recognize the kinds of strangers who tend to show up at certain times, in certain markets, in certain situations, and you can begin to position yourself accordingly.

The naive view is that markets hold two groups. The smart money, meaning institutions and hedge funds and the whales, and the dumb money, meaning you. The smart money knows things. The dumb money guesses. The whole game, in this view, is just figuring out what the smart money is doing and copying it.

This view is both true and dangerously incomplete.

True, because there are sophisticated participants in every market, they collectively have informational, technological, and capital advantages over you, and you should respect those advantages. Dangerously incomplete, because it imagines the market as one tribe of them against one tribe of us, when in fact the market is more like a crowded international airport. Dozens of groups, each there for a different reason, each on a different clock, each measuring success differently. The cargo pilot does not care what the honeymooners are doing. The honeymooners do not care about the air-traffic controllers. The cleaning crew does not care about any of it. They are all in the same building, all making decisions, and the building somehow functions.

A market is the building. The participants are everyone in it.

In a futures market, the people in the building sort into roughly five categories. Learn these five, and you have a more useful mental model than ninety percent of retail traders, because most retail traders never sit down and think about it at all. They stare at the chart and feel things. Marcus, on Tuesday, was staring at the chart and feeling things.

Let us go to the airport and meet everyone.

The Hedger: The Person Who Actually Needs the Stuff

The first and oldest participant is the commercial hedger. The hedger is the reason futures markets exist, and you should hold a small amount of professional respect for the hedger at all times. Without the hedger, there is no market. Without the market, you are not reading this book.

A hedger is somebody whose actual business is exposed to the price of the thing being traded, and who uses the futures market to manage that exposure. The classic example is the corn farmer. Here is a real one.

Walt grows corn on 1,400 acres in Iowa. It is May. He has just finished planting. Between now and October, his costs are mostly locked in: fertilizer, seed, fuel, the loan payment on the combine. He knows roughly how many bushels he will harvest, give or take a hailstorm. What he does not know is what those bushels will be worth in October.

Right now December corn futures trade at $4.80 a bushel. At $4.80, Walt does the math and figures he clears a modest but acceptable profit. If corn is $5.40 in October, he has a fantastic year. If corn is $3.90, he cannot pay his loan.

Walt has a choice. He can take his chances and find out in October, or he can sell some of his expected harvest right now, at $4.80, by selling December corn futures. He does not have the corn yet. He is promising to deliver it. If corn is $5.40 in October, he loses on the futures position, since he sold at $4.80 and the market is now $5.40, a 60-cent loss, but he wins on his actual crop, which he sells at $5.40. The two cancel. If corn is $3.90 in October, he wins on the futures position, a 90-cent gain, and loses on the crop. Again they cancel.

Walt has not maximized his upside. He has done something far more valuable to a man with a multi-million-dollar loan against a combine. He has eliminated his variance. He has converted "I do not know what I will make this year" into "I know what I will make this year." The futures contract, for Walt, is not a bet. It is insurance.

On the other side of Walt's trade is a man named Karl. Karl works for a Midwestern cereal company that will need to buy corn in October to make breakfast cereal. Karl has Walt's problem in reverse. If corn is $5.40 in October, his company gets crushed. If it is $3.90, they have a great year. Karl, also in May, also at $4.80, buys December corn futures. He has locked in his input cost. Same move as Walt, converting variance into certainty, from the other side.

Walt and Karl are both hedgers. On their futures positions, collectively, they make and lose nothing on net, because the gain on one side equals the loss on the other. What they have done is take price risk out of their businesses and into a market where other people will bear it.

Why does this matter to you, the speculator who has never seen a bushel of corn?

Because hedgers are the slow, deep current of the market, they move on weather, on crop reports, on planting intentions, on harvest progress, on cattle inventories, on ethanol demand. They do not care about your daily chart. They are placing large, persistent orders driven by the real economy, and over weeks and months their collective behavior is one of the most powerful forces shaping the long-term trend of any commodity contract.

When a USDA report drops at 11 a.m. on a Thursday, and the corn market shudders, that is not speculators. That is tens of thousands of Walts and Karls, plus the desks that serve them, recalculating their hedges in real time. If you do not know that report exists, you are on the wrong side of the move before the algorithm finishes parsing the headline.

The hedger's signature: large, persistent, slow-developing flow, concentrated around scheduled fundamental events, almost completely indifferent to short-term price action.

The Speculator: The Person Who Wants to Make Money

The second participant is the speculator. The speculator has no underlying business reason to be in the market. He is there for one reason: to make money on price changes. This is the camp Marcus just joined, and the camp you are joining.

The speculator camp is enormous and varied. It includes retail day traders with accounts from $5,000 to $5 million, trading from a spare bedroom or an office. It includes hedge funds, from two-person discretionary shops to multi-billion-dollar global macro firms with satellite-imagery contracts and physicists on the payroll. It includes Commodity Trading Advisors running systematic trend programs across dozens of contracts at once, often holding for weeks. It includes proprietary trading firms, private partnerships where mathematicians, engineers, and ex-poker players trade the firm's own capital with algorithms you cannot see and would not understand. It includes high-frequency firms that hold positions for milliseconds, take pennies on millions of trades, and have built their server racks inside the exchange's data center because the speed of light is too slow. It includes family offices managing inherited wealth, and sovereign wealth funds quietly hedging country-level exposures.

And, in growing numbers, it includes a newer kind of speculator who trades a firm's capital without ever working at the firm. This is Dani. She passed, or is trying to pass, an evaluation that lets her trade a proprietary shop's money under a fixed set of rules, keeping most of what she makes. She is a speculator in every technical sense, but with one difference that changes her behavior on every single trade: the money is not hers, the rules are not hers, and a loss limit she did not write can end her account at a level she would never have stopped at on her own. That difference is invisible on the chart and decisive in the outcome. Hold onto it. It is the entire reason the back half of this book exists, and it is why Dani keeps failing for reasons Marcus has not even met yet.

What unites all of them is one fact. They are in the market for profit, not for hedging. They are speculators in the technical sense, those who take on price risk in exchange for the possibility of price gain.

Speculators get called parasites by people who do not understand markets. This is silly. Without speculators, the hedgers have no one to trade with. Walt cannot sell his corn forward at $4.80 if nobody will buy it. Karl cannot lock his cost if nobody will sell. The speculator is the counterparty to the hedge. The speculator absorbs the price risk the farmer and the cereal company want to shed, and in exchange hopes to be paid for it.

The speculator's signature: faster time horizons, from milliseconds to weeks, reaction to both fundamental events and technical signals, willingness to flip direction quickly, and a tendency to cluster at the same price levels, because most speculators are looking at the same charts. Remember that last part. It will matter when we talk about where stops get hunted.

You are about to become a member of this group. Welcome. The dress code is whatever you happen to be wearing.

The Arbitrageur: The Person Who Makes Sure 1 + 1 = 2

The third participant is the arbitrageur, the silent custodian who walks the market every nanosecond, making sure nothing is mispriced relative to anything else.

Here is what arbitrage looks like. Gold trades on the COMEX futures exchange. Gold also trades in physical form in London vaults, in ETF form on the New York Stock Exchange, and in spot form between banks worldwide. In theory, all these prices track each other almost perfectly, because they all reference the same metal. In practice, for tiny fractions of a second, they do not. The futures contract might tick up two cents while spot has not moved. The ETF might lag the futures by a hundredth of a percent.

The arbitrageur's job, now almost entirely done by algorithms, is to detect these gaps and trade them away. The instant futures go up two cents relative to spot, the arbitrageur sells futures and buys spot. The buying pushes spot up, the selling pushes futures down, the gap closes, and the arbitrageur captures a tiny riskless profit. Multiply by ten thousand times a day across every related instrument in the world, and you have a small but reliable business.

You are never going to be an arbitrageur. The opportunities last microseconds, the technology costs millions, the margins are razor thin. But you should know they exist, because they explain something important. Markets are aggressively efficient at the micro level and surprisingly inefficient at the macro level.

Efficient at the micro level means any obvious mechanical mispricing, between gold futures and gold spot, between an ETF and its basket, gets eaten by an algorithm within milliseconds. There is no free money on the sidewalk. If you ever think "this seems too easy, why is everyone not doing it," the answer is almost always that everyone is doing it, faster than you can imagine, and the opportunity is a mirage.

Inefficient at the macro level means the questions humans have to interpret: what does this jobs report mean for the Fed, what does the new tariff policy do to soybean demand, is the trend in oil over, an algorithm cannot solve those. They are messy, they require judgment, they require time, and that is where the speculator's edge lives.

The arbitrageur takes the obvious money. The speculator takes the interpretive money—different jobs.

The arbitrageur's signature: invisible to you, everywhere in the data, responsible for the eerie efficiency of intraday price relationships, and the reason obvious mispricings rarely actually exist.

The Market Maker: The Person Who Will Always Trade With You

The fourth participant is the market maker, the reason you can buy or sell anything, ever, at any moment of the day.

A market maker is a firm, rarely a human now, whose entire business is always to quote both a bid and an ask on a specific contract. If you want to buy, they will sell to you. If you want to sell, they will buy from you. They are the house, in the most literal sense. They take the other side of every trade no one else happens to be on the other side of.

How do they make money? Through the bid-ask spread, which we dig into properly in Chapter 3. In essence, they buy a little lower than they sell. If the bid is 4,832.00 and the ask is 4,832.25, the market maker will buy from you at 4,832.00 and sell to you at 4,832.25. Do that a million times a day while staying roughly balanced, and you pocket the spread on every round trip. It is a brutal, capital-intensive, technology-heavy business that pays in pennies and demands extreme discipline. The firms that do it well are some of the most profitable companies in finance you have never heard of.

The market maker has no opinion on direction and does not want to be long or short overnight. The market maker wants to flatten its book by the end of each session, having captured the spread on as many trades as possible. In a deep sense, it is the most professional participant in the ecosystem, and the one retail traders take most for granted.

Why this matters to you: every time you place a market order in a liquid contract, and it fills instantly at the displayed price, you are interacting with a market maker. The reason you can trade at 3 a.m. on a Tuesday is that a market maker kept its quotes live. The reason the spread on the E-mini is one tick wide is that several market makers are competing to be the one you trade with. And when liquidity disappears, when the bid-ask suddenly yawns open in a panic, what you are watching is market makers stepping back because the risk of being run over has exceeded the pennies they expect to earn.

The market maker's signature: always there, never directional, captures the spread, vanishes when things get scary. Treat them as the infrastructure of the market, not as participants in your trade.

The Algorithm: The Sixth Person Who Was Not on the List

I told you there are five categories. I shaded the truth. There is a sixth, less a category than a substrate running underneath the other five.

The sixth participant is the algorithm, and it is, increasingly, doing the work of all the others. Algorithms calculate the hedger's adjustments. The speculator's entries and exits, for all but a small minority of discretionary humans, are executed by algorithms. The arbitrageur is an algorithm. Algorithms run the market maker. The retail trader who hits a button is routed through an algorithm that decides where to send the order. The exchange that matches the buy and the sell is an algorithm. It is algorithms all the way down.

This is not a doom point. It is a structural one. The market you are about to trade is not a room full of yelling men in colored jackets, the image Sal came up with inside, and the one most beginners still carry. It is a fluorescent-lit data center. It is silent. The decisions are made in code no human reads in real time. The latency between your decision and the market's reaction is measured in microseconds.

The practical implication: do not expect markets to behave the way a market full of humans would. Algorithms do not panic, but they do stop. They have risk limits and circuit breakers, and when those trigger, the algorithm withdraws. This is why markets sometimes appear to fall through levels in milliseconds with no apparent buyers. The buyers, algorithms all, simultaneously concluded the risk had changed and pulled their bids. There is nobody at the wheel because there was never anybody at the wheel.

This sounds terrifying, and on its worst days it is. But it is also a deep reason the human discretionary trader still has a job. At the interpretive layer, where the question is what does this news mean, algorithms struggle. They get faster every year, but the meaning of things- should I be aggressive here, or careful, or out entirely- remains a place a clear-headed human can compete. Not because the human is faster. Because the human can change his mind for the right reason, hold that phrase, clear-headed, lightly for now. The whole of Trade Calm is about the fact that the human across from the algorithm is usually anything but, and that being the calm one in a market of panicking humans is itself an edge.

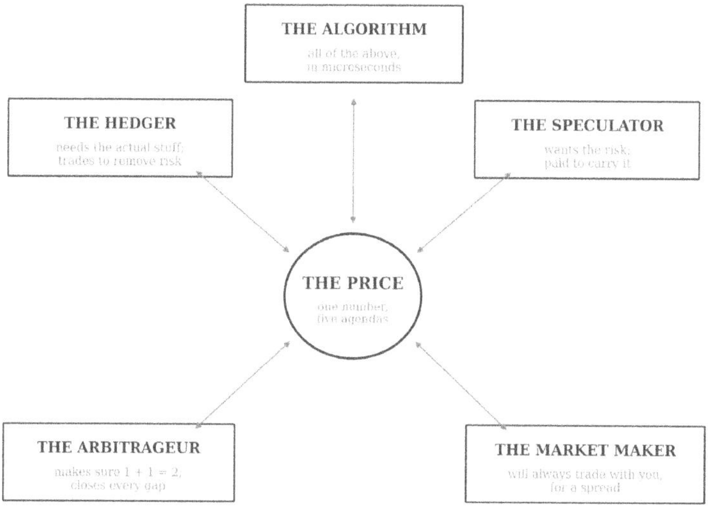

The five kinds of strangers on the other side of your trade. Every fill is two of them disagreeing about the next revision.

Putting the Five (Six) Together: How a Price Actually Happens

Now put them all in the room and watch them make a price.

It is 8:29:55 a.m. Eastern on the first Friday of the month. The Bureau of Labor Statistics is about to release nonfarm payrolls—the E-mini S&P 500 future trades at 4,832.50. Consensus is 187,000 jobs added. Somewhere, in a spare bedroom, Marcus is watching, because his cousin told him the jobs number is "where the money is," and Marcus has a position he probably should not have. Somewhere else, Dani is watching the same clock, flat, because the rules of the evaluation she is days into make a 187,000-job lottery ticket exactly the kind of trade that ends accounts, and she has finally, expensively, learned to sit out the print.

In the five seconds before the release: the hedgers, pension funds, insurers, corporate treasurers, adjusted earlier in the week on longer-term views and are quiet now. The speculators are stacked on both sides, longs betting strong, shorts betting weak, many flat and simply watching. The arbitrageurs are watching twenty correlated instruments at once. The market makers have widened their spreads in anticipation, bid 4,832.25, ask 4,832.75, charging more for liquidity because they are about to be run over by one side or the other. The algorithms underneath all of it have parsing engines on standby, ready to read the wire and translate it into orders in microseconds.

At 8:30:00.000, the report releases. 143,000 jobs. Far below consensus.

What happens in the next 250 milliseconds: the parsing algorithms read the headline and immediately submit sell orders in equity futures and buy orders in Treasury futures, since weaker jobs means the Fed might cut sooner, which means bonds rally and stocks first jump on the rate-cut hope then often sell off on growth fears. The market does both at once. The market makers, hit by a wave on one side, pull their quotes and re-post wider, and the E-mini spread blows out to five ticks for a moment. The arbitrageurs re-price the relationships between the S&P, Nasdaq, and Russell futures, the ETFs, implied volatility, and the dollar, tiny gaps opening and closing in nanoseconds. The discretionary humans- this is Marcus, and someday a steadier version of you- watch it unfold and decide whether to take the trade they planned. Some hit the button. Some wait. Some change their minds because the price action does not look right. The hedgers, mostly, sit still and rebalance later.

Within thirty seconds, the price has found a new equilibrium. Within five minutes the spread is back to one tick. Within an hour the headlines are out, the analysts have published, and the slower money is starting to move.

What you just watched was a price discovered by a heterogeneous crowd, each member with a different goal, a different clock, a different toolkit, and a different reason to be there. That is what a market is. Not a single intelligence. Not a tribe. An ecosystem.

Marcus, by the way, lost money on the print. He had guessed direction, and the market did the thing markets love most: it went his way for four seconds and then reversed and took out his stop. He did not yet understand that he had been the slowest, least-informed participant in a room full of professionals and machines, holding a position for a reason he could not have defended out loud. Dani, flat, lost nothing, which inside an evaluation is its own kind of winning. We will fix Marcus. It starts with knowing the room exists.

What This Means for You

The practical implication of all of this is important enough to put plainly. You are not trading against "the market." You are trading against a specific population of other participants, and its composition changes by the second.

This is not philosophy. It has consequences. Trade an agricultural commodity around a USDA report, and you are mostly competing with hedger flow and the algorithms parsing the report. You are not smarter than the market. You are betting your reading of the report agrees with what the next ten minutes of flow will do. Trade an index future in a thin overnight session, and you are mostly competing with market makers and a few other speculators. The price can move on remarkably small flow because almost nobody is home. Trade through a Fed announcement and you are competing with everyone, at maximum speed, with maximum capital, in a window of seconds. You will lose to the algorithms on speed. You can only win on interpretation. Trade at 2 p.m. on a quiet Wednesday in a major contract, and the flow is mostly speculators making small adjustments and market makers earning the spread. Volatility is low because the participants are idling.

Knowing who is in the room, and being honest about how that population shifts from hour to hour and event to event, is a more durable edge than any indicator you will ever learn. It is the difference between guessing and knowing.

And to know who is in the room, you have to understand the room itself. How prices form. How the bid and the ask move. What volume actually represents. Why some prices stick, and others slide right through. How the plumbing works.

That is Chapter 3.

CHAPTER 2, KEY IDEAS

- **Every trade has a counterparty, and the counterparty is never random.** Five, or really six, categories populate every market: hedgers, speculators, arbitrageurs, market makers, and the algorithms running under all of them.
- **Hedgers create the slow, deep current** of long-term trends. They move on real-world fundamentals and care nothing for your chart.
- **Speculators are the camp you are joining,** and the fastest-growing corner of it is the funded trader on a firm's capital. Dani trades like a speculator with one decisive twist: rules she did not write, on money that is not hers, that change what a loss is allowed to cost.
- **Arbitrageurs are the silent custodians.** They eat obvious mispricings in microseconds, which is why free money on the table rarely actually exists.
- **Market makers are the infrastructure.** They quote both sides, earn the spread, and disappear when things get scary. They are why you can trade at 3 a.m. and why the spread widens in a panic.
- **"Smart money vs. dumb money" is a lazy model.** The real one is a heterogeneous ecosystem where different participants have different goals at different times. Your edge comes from knowing who you are trading against right now. On his first big print, Marcus was the slowest participant in the room and did not know it. Dani, flat by rule, lost nothing, which inside an evaluation is a win.

CHAPTER 3

The Plumbing

A week into trading, Marcus did something that cost him eleven dollars and taught him more than any video had.

He wanted out of a losing crude oil position, fast, so he hit the market sell button the way you slam a door. The fill came back a few cents worse than the price glowing on his screen a half-second earlier. Eleven dollars, gone, to nobody he could name. He had not been wrong about direction in that instant. He had been wrong about a thing underneath the chart that he did not know existed. He emailed Sal, whom he had started talking to in a futures forum, a single confused line: "Where did the money go?" Sal wrote back two words. "The plumbing."

You can spend years staring at a chart and never really understand what the chart is of.

Nobody warns beginners about this. You open a trading app, you see green and red candles marching across the screen, and you assume, reasonably, that you are looking at the price. The single, authoritative number out there in the world called "the price of crude oil," displayed for you.

There is no such number. There is, at every instant, a cluster of prices: bids, asks, recent fills, larger resting orders just behind the front of the queue. What your chart shows is a heavily summarized photograph of one slice of that cluster, taken once per bar, with most of the detail thrown away.

Until you understand what is under that photograph, you are trading blind. You are reading a weather map without knowing what an isobar is. You will pick up some patterns by trial and error, but you will never know why the weather does what it does, which means the weather will keep surprising you. It surprised Marcus for eleven dollars. It surprises some people for a great deal more.

This chapter is the plumbing. The bid-ask, volume, the order book, liquidity, and the way prices actually move from one number to the next. None of it is glamorous. All of it is fundamental. Skip it, and you will pay for skipping it later, in a currency I assume you would rather keep.

Two Prices, Always

At every moment of the trading day, every active futures contract has two prices. Not one. Two.

The first is the bid, the highest price any willing buyer is currently offering to pay. It is a standing offer: I will pay X for this contract right now, if anyone wants to sell to me.

The second is the ask, sometimes called the offer, the lowest price any willing seller is currently offering to accept. The mirror image: I will sell this contract for Y right now, if anyone wants to buy from me.

The bid is always lower than the ask. If the bid were ever higher than the ask, the two orders would match and execute instantly. They cannot coexist. So there is always a small gap between them, the bid-ask spread, and that gap is the cost of trading immediately.

Here is the rule you will use ten thousand times in your career:

> **If you want to buy right now, you pay the ask. If you want to sell right now, you receive the bid.**

That is the whole mechanism. Every market order you place obeys it. Every fill is at one of these two prices. When Marcus slammed the sell button, he received the bid, which was a touch below the last price he had seen, and the difference was his eleven dollars.

Picture an auction house with two auctioneers shouting at once. The first is shouting "who will bid forty-eight thirty-two," and a hundred buyers are nodding. The second is shouting "who will take forty-eight thirty-two and a quarter," and a hundred sellers are nodding. Walk in and shout "I want to buy now," and the second auctioneer matches you with a seller at 4,832.25. Shout "I want to sell now," and the first matches you with a buyer at 4,832.00. The quarter-point difference goes to nobody. It is the friction of the system, and its name is the spread.

The Bid-Ask Spread Is a Tax

Every time you trade, you pay the spread. There is no avoiding it.

Buy a contract at the ask and immediately sell it back at the bid, and you have not broken even. You have lost the spread. On one E-mini S&P contract, where a tick is $12.50, a one-tick spread costs $12.50 on every round trip. Do twenty round trips a day and you have paid $250 a day in spread alone. Over a year of trading days, that is north of $60,000, and you have not yet paid your broker, the exchange, or the clearing firm.

This is not a small detail. It is one of the most important numbers in your trading life. The spread is a tax on every trade. The more often you trade, the more you pay. The wider the spread on the contract you choose, the more you pay. The choice of which contract to trade is, almost entirely, a choice of how much spread tax you can stomach. It is also, quietly, one of the reasons over-trading kills evaluation accounts. Every extra round trip a bored trader takes to "stay active" is another tax payment against a fixed profit target.

The most liquid contracts in the world, the E-mini S&P 500, the 10-year Treasury note, crude oil, gold, usually have spreads of one tick. That is as good as it gets. You pay that tax once per round trip and barely notice. Less liquid contracts, secondary agricultural products, thinly traded currencies, certain short-end rate contracts, can run three, five, or ten ticks wide. On those you can be right about direction and still lose money, because the spread you paid to get in is bigger than the move you caught.

The general rule: trade the most liquid version of whatever you want to trade. There is no prize for being clever about which contract you pick. The prize is paid in dollars at the end of the year, and the spread tax is one of the easiest ways to lose those dollars without ever being wrong about a single trade.

Volume: The Truth of the Move

If the bid-ask tells you what the market is willing to do, volume tells you what it is actually doing.

Volume is the number of contracts traded in a given period. Easy definition, slightly harder concept, because not all price moves are equal. A price can move from 4,830 to 4,835 on five contracts, a tiny puff of activity, easily reversed, meaning almost nothing. Or it can move the same five points on fifty thousand contracts, a wall of conviction, hard to undo, meaning a great many participants just changed their minds at once. The chart shows the same five-point move both times. The volume tells you whether it meant anything.

This is why professionals watch volume as obsessively as price. The market believes a move on heavy volume. Real money went behind the direction, and it is unlikely to reverse on a dime. A move on light volume is merely suspected; not enough participants confirmed it, and it tends to get unwound fast.

A few relationships show up often enough to be worth keeping. Rising prices on rising volume is the textbook signature of a strong uptrend, new money agreeing with the direction, and these tend to persist. Rising prices on falling volume is a weakening uptrend, fewer and fewer buyers willing to chase, and it often precedes a reversal because the buying is exhausting itself. Falling prices on rising volume is the mirror, a downtrend validated by participation. And a sharp move on an enormous volume spike is often the climax of a trend rather than its continuation, the moment the last holdouts capitulate and the move runs out of fuel because there is nobody left to convince. The blow-off top and the selling climax are both volume signatures as much as price ones.

You will develop a feel for this with reps. A candle that closes strong on heavy volume looks different from one that closes strong on weak volume, even though they are identical on a chart with no volume pane. Once you start watching, you cannot unsee it.

The Order Book: Watching the Crowd Form

Above the bid and ask, every modern futures platform shows the order book, or the depth of market, the DOM. The order book shows the queue: how many contracts are resting at each price level, waiting to trade.

This is where it gets interesting. Say the E-mini is trading 4,832.25 ask, 4,832.00 bid. Above the ask, the book might show 1,247 contracts at 4,832.50, 894 at 4,832.75, 2,103 at 4,833.00, 678 at 4,833.25. Below the bid, 1,156 at 4,831.75, 998 at 4,831.50, 2,847 at 4,831.25, 540 at 4,831.00.

You are looking at resting limit orders, orders not currently aggressive (or they would have matched already) but sitting there, waiting to absorb whatever aggressive buying or selling comes through.

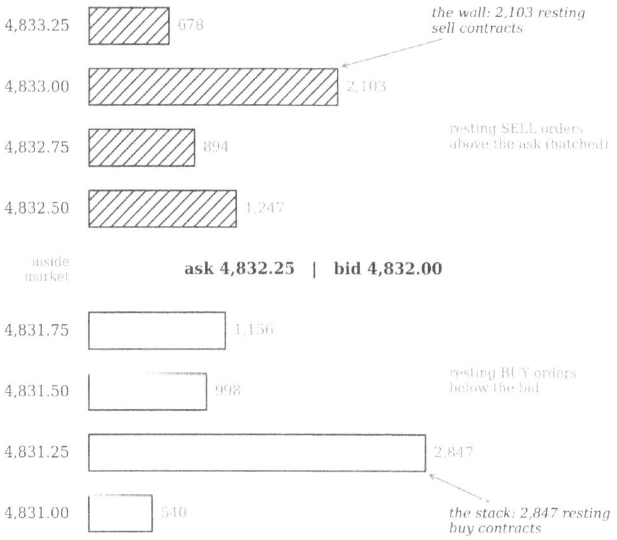

The order book around one inside market. The wall and the stack act as short-term ceiling and floor, right up until they vanish.

Notice the numbers are not uniform. There is a big stack at 4,833.00 and another at 4,831.25. Those concentrations act as short-term resistance and support. If price climbs toward 4,833.00, it runs into a 2,103-contract wall, and the market needs enough aggressive buyers to absorb those before it can push higher. Sometimes it does. Sometimes it cannot, and price stalls. This is the moment-to-moment microstructure of a market. Levels appear, get tested, get absorbed or hold, then fall away or get reinforced. Good short-term traders read the DOM the way a poker player reads a table, not as truth exactly, but as one more piece of information that sharpens the estimate of what is about to happen.

Dani learned to read the DOM the hard way, which is the only way. Early in her second evaluation, she watched a 3,000-contract wall sit on the offer just above her entry and decided it was a ceiling, so she sized up a short into it, certain the wall would hold. The wall vanished the instant price arrived, the way the biggest walls often do, because it was never real. It was a spoof, a large order placed to fake a level and pulled before it could ever be filled. Price tore straight through the space, her stop slipped, and a trade she had built around a number on the screen cost her three times what she had planned. Sal, when she told him, did not lecture. He said, "The book is a rumor, not a receipt. Trade what fills, not what is resting." She wrote it on a sticky note. It is still on her monitor.

A warning, then, because it is the same one: the order book lies. Or more precisely, it gets gamed. Algorithms place large spoof orders at certain levels to fake support or resistance, then pull them the instant price approaches. Spoofing is illegal in most jurisdictions and gets prosecuted occasionally, but it lives on in less prosecutable variants every day. Do not treat the DOM as gospel. Treat it as one input, useful especially when it agrees with recent trading, never a crystal ball.

Liquidity: Your Trading Lifeline

We have used the word liquidity several times without defining it. Liquidity is the ease with which you can buy or sell a meaningful quantity without moving the price against yourself.

Think of it as the depth of the pool you are about to jump into. A liquid market is a deep pool. You can dive in, make a big splash, and the water absorbs it. An illiquid market is a kiddie pool. You can dive in once, but you are going to feel the bottom, and so is everyone else, and you have now ruined the pool for the room.

In a liquid market, spreads are tight, often one tick. The book is deep on both sides, thousands of contracts across many levels. You can place a market order for a hundred contracts and barely move price.

You can enter at one price and exit moments later at essentially the same one. Slippage, the difference between the price you expected and the price you got, is minimal.

In an illiquid market, spreads are wide, sometimes ten ticks or more. The book is thin and irregular, small clusters separated by gaps. A modest market order sweeps through several levels, getting worse fills as it goes. Entering and exiting takes work, sometimes a limit order and a wait, and sometimes you do not get filled at all. And slippage is brutal. A trade you thought carried $50 of risk costs you $300 because your stop, when it triggered, swept through three empty levels before finding a buyer. That sentence is not hypothetical. It is exactly how a controlled loss becomes an uncontrolled one, and it is half of what killed the trader in the next chapter, and most of what blew up Dani's spoof trade above.

The liquidity of a contract is the single most important property to weigh when choosing what to trade. I cannot say it strongly enough. A great strategy in an illiquid market becomes a bad strategy, because the friction eats the edge. A mediocre strategy in a deeply liquid market can still pay, because the friction is small enough to ignore.

The most liquid futures contracts today are roughly the E-mini S&P 500 (ES), the king of equity index futures, with millions of contracts a day; the 10-year Treasury note (ZN), the benchmark rate contract; crude oil (CL), deeply liquid in U.S. and European hours and thinner overnight; the E-mini Nasdaq 100 (NQ), the high-volatility cousin of the ES; gold (GC), extremely liquid in U.S. hours; and Euro FX (6E), the most liquid currency future. Trade these, and a handful of other top-tier contracts, and liquidity will not be your problem. Wander into the thinly traded ones, obscure agricultural products, long-end rate futures, micro versions of niche indices. You will find the spread you pay and the slippage you suffer can quietly turn a winning system into a losing one.

Price Discovery: How the Market Makes Up Its Mind

So far, the static picture. Bid, ask, spread, volume, liquidity. Now, how prices actually change.

The process by which a market arrives at a new price is called price discovery, and it is one of the more elegant things humans have built, even when machines are doing all of it.

It works roughly like this. New information arrives, anything from a scheduled report to a surprise headline to a large hedger order to a technical break to a central banker's offhand remark. Participants interpret it, each with their own model and incentives. The hedger asks whether it changes their exposure, the speculator whether it creates an opportunity, the arbitrageur whether it creates a mispricing, the market maker whether it changes the risk of quoting. The interpretations turn into orders. Some buy, some sell, some pull existing orders, some place new ones, some do nothing, and the book changes in real time. Aggressive orders consume resting ones, buyers at market taking out the resting offers, sellers at market taking out the resting bids, and the spread shifts to reflect the new state of the queue. A new price is reached, sometimes a hair from the old one, sometimes a violent re-pricing far away. Then the process repeats, continuously, forever, because information never stops arriving. There is no settled price. There is only the most recent transaction, already obsolete by the time you read it.

The implication is that prices are not facts. They are estimates. The market constantly estimates the value of the contract from everything it currently knows, and revises that estimate without pause. When a news event hits, and price moves $400, you are watching the market revise in real time. The new price is not more correct than the old one. It is the current best guess, by the current crowd, under the current information. Tomorrow it gets revised again.

This is why "the market is always right" is one of the more annoying truisms in trading. The market is not right. The market is current. There is a meaningful difference. The market that priced gasoline near $1.80 a gallon in the spring of 2020 was current. The market that priced it near $5.00 in 2022 was current. The market that priced Lehman Brothers at $20 in the summer of 2008 was current. None of those prices were correct. They were the best estimates the crowd could make at the time, with what the crowd had. Your job is not to argue with the current price. Your job is to figure out, more often than not, which direction the next revision is likely to go.

Market Orders, Limit Orders, and the Difference That Matters

When you place a trade, your platform offers two basic order types, plus a half-dozen exotic ones.

A market order says: fill me right now, at whatever the best available price is. Submit a market buy, and it matches the best resting ask and fills immediately. If that ask does not hold enough contracts to fill you, you sweep up through the book, filling at progressively higher prices, until you have your size. A market order guarantees execution. It does not guarantee price. In a liquid contract during normal hours, this barely matters; you fill within a tick of where you expected. In an illiquid contract, or during a fast event, the gap between the price you wanted and the price you got can be enormous. That gap is slippage, and slippage is what turns a market order from a convenience into a hazard. It is what got Marcus for eleven dollars, and it is what gets other people for eleven hundred.

A limit order says: fill me only at this price, or better. Submit a limit buy at 4,832.00, and you will not pay more than 4,832.00. If the market never trades there or lower, your order sits unfilled. A limit order guarantees price. It does not guarantee execution. You might place one and watch the market walk away without ever filling you, leaving you with nothing: no trade, no position, no opportunity.

The choice comes down to one question: what do I care about more, certainty of execution or certainty of price? For most situations: entering a trade that depends on a specific level, use a limit order; you would rather miss it than pay ten extra ticks chasing it. Exiting because something has gone wrong, your stop triggered, the market did something you did not expect, use a market order; you would rather take a slightly worse price than stay stuck in a position that is bleeding. Exiting at a planned profit target: use a limit order, since the whole point of the target is the specific price.

There are refinements. Stop orders that become market orders at a trigger price, stop-limit orders that become limit orders at a trigger, time-in-force settings, bracket orders that pre-set your target and stop the moment you enter. We will return to the useful ones as we need them. For now: market orders guarantee execution but not price; limit orders guarantee price but not execution. Internalize the difference before it teaches you the way it taught Marcus.

The Electronic Market: What Is Actually Going On

The image many people still carry of futures trading is the floor. Men in colored jackets, hand signals, paper tickets, shouting. It is a charming image, and Sal can tell you it was real. It is also, now, almost entirely historical.

The futures markets you and I will trade are electronic. A few open-outcry pits survive in corners for a few contracts, but the volume has moved overwhelmingly to electronic platforms, Globex for the CME contracts, ICE for the ICE contracts, and so on. In practice, this means speed, orders executing in microseconds, with the latency between your click and your fill on a decent retail setup in the tens of milliseconds, while the professionals operate in single-digit microseconds from servers parked inside the exchange's data center. It means transparency, the full order book visible to anyone with a market-data feed, which was not true a generation ago. It means mostly equal access, a retail trader with a good platform seeing the same price stream as a hedge fund, the fund still holding advantages in data, connection speed, capital, and algorithms, but the price you see being the price they see, no privileged feed. And it means near-24-hour markets that do not wait for you to wake up.

The implication for a new trader is sobering. You are entering a market thoroughly optimized by participants who are smarter, faster, better capitalized, and better equipped than you. You will not outspeed them. You will not out-engineer them. You will not get an information edge on a scheduled economic release.

What you can have is patience, discipline, the willingness to wait for high-probability setups, and the cold-blooded ability to take losses without letting them metastasize. Those are not advantages technology can copy; they are virtues. The market is full of impatient, undisciplined, hopeful traders who will gladly take the other side of your patient, disciplined trade. Your edge is not over the algorithms. Your edge is over the other humans. And inside an evaluation, where every participant is a small, undercapitalized human fighting the same rules, that edge is the entire game.

That is a livable edge, but only if you respect what the plumbing is doing every microsecond of every day. The bid and ask are not abstract; they are the actual prices at which you can transact right now. The order book is not decoration, it is the queue you are about to join. Volume is not a footnote; it is the truth-detector for everything else on the chart.

Master the plumbing and the rest of trading becomes a series of decisions you can make with clear eyes. Skip it, and you will spend years wondering why the chart keeps lying to you. It is not lying. You are misreading it.

In the next chapter we begin to fix that by tackling the single most important concept in the entire book, the one that, more than any other, separates the traders who survive from the ones who do not.

Risk.

CHAPTER 3, KEY IDEAS

- **There is no single price. There are always two:** the bid, the best a buyer will pay, and the ask, the best a seller will accept. The gap between them is the spread, and the spread is a tax you pay on every trade. Marcus paid it the first time he slammed a market order.
- **Volume is the truth-detector.** A move on heavy volume is real; a move on light volume is suspect. Read price and volume together, or you are reading half the data.
- **The order book is a rumor, not a receipt.** Resting orders stack at each level and create short-term support and resistance, but the biggest walls are often spoofs that vanish on contact. Trade what fills, not what is resting. It cost Dani an evaluation to learn it.
- **Liquidity is your trading lifeline.** A liquid market lets you enter and exit without moving price against yourself. An illiquid one punishes you for trading at all, and turns a controlled stop into an uncontrolled loss. Stick to the most liquid version of any asset class you trade.
- **Price discovery is continuous, not occasional.** The market is always digesting something, and the current price is just the

latest estimate by the current crowd. The market is not always right. It is always current.

- **Market orders guarantee execution, not price. Limit orders guarantee price, not execution.** Choose deliberately. Market orders to escape, limit orders to enter, neither casually.
- **You will not out-speed the algorithms. You can out-discipline the other humans.** That is the edge actually available to you, and inside an evaluation, where everyone is fighting the same rules, it is the whole game.

CHAPTER 4

The Only Chapter That Matters

It is 11:47 on a Wednesday morning, and Marcus is about to make the most expensive decision of his short trading life.

He does not know that yet. From where he sits, it does not feel like a decision at all. It feels like patience.

Marcus is thirty-four. He has a spare bedroom in a rented townhouse, two monitors he paid too much for, a coffee that went cold an hour ago, and a crude oil position that is not doing what he was so certain it would do. He went long one contract an hour ago at $70.25, because the chart said up and his gut agreed, and for about nine minutes he was right. Then he was wrong. The price is $69.95 now and sliding, and his stop, the stop he set with a clear head before he entered, the one that says get me out at $69.85, is ten cents away.

His finger is resting on the mouse. The cursor is hovering over the stop order. And a voice in his head, calm, reasonable, weirdly persuasive, is explaining to him that the smart move, the patient move, the move a real trader would make, is to give the trade a little more room.

We are going to leave Marcus there. Finger on the mouse, voice in his ear, ten cents from his stop. Hold him in your mind for the length of this chapter, because what he does in the next ninety seconds is the entire subject of it, and most of the rest of this book is scaffolding around this single moment.

If you were forced, at gunpoint, in a particularly literary mugging, to read only one chapter of this book, this is the one I would point you to. Not the chapters on chart patterns. Not the chapters on strategy. Not even the chapter on the inner game, which is where most other books in this genre promise the magic lives. This one. The risk chapter.

The reason is simple and unforgiving. Every other skill in this book depends on this chapter being true in your hands, not in the abstract, in your actual hands, at 11:47 on an actual Wednesday. You can own the cleanest entry technique on the street and the best chart-reading eye in your time zone, and if you are wrong about risk, you will blow up your account anyway. You can be the most disciplined analyst in your trading group and blow up your account anyway. There is no edge, no insight, no system, and no amount of grinding work that compensates for being wrong about risk. And there is no evaluation, no funded account, no payout, that survives it for a week. Every rule a prop firm will ever test you on is just this chapter, enforced by someone else.

So put down your phone. Tell the person in the next room you will be a while. This one matters.

The Man Who Could Not Take the Loss

Before Marcus, there was Cooper.

I knew a trader I will call Cooper. In the technical sense, Cooper was very good. He had a system. He had back-tested it. He understood market structure better than I did at the time; he could read the order book and see what the algorithms were doing, and he could place an entry inside a one-tick window. If you had asked anyone who knew him to name the person most likely to get rich trading, the answer was Cooper.

Cooper had one weakness, which he was aware of and openly joked about. He hated taking losses. Specifically, he hated taking losses on trades he *knew* were eventually going to work. When a trade went against him, he would tell himself a story: the move was a fake-out, the real direction was the one he had called, and anyone with the patience to sit through a little noise would be rewarded. He did not exactly move his stop. He would, sometimes, cancel it. And then re-enter it a little lower. And then cancel that one.

For about eighteen months, this worked. Or it appeared to. Most of the time, the market did come back, Cooper would sit through a drawdown that should have stopped him out, the trade would turn, and he would close a small winner. The lesson he absorbed, the wrong lesson, the lethal one, was that his instinct was right and the stops were the problem. The stops were keeping him from his profits.

You can see where this is going, because you have a chart of it in your head already. One spring, Cooper was long a contract. It went against him. He canceled the stop. It went further against him. He averaged down. It went further against him. He averaged down again. By the close that Tuesday, he was down forty percent of his account on a single position, and he held it overnight, telling himself the close was a fake-out and the morning would fix it.

The morning gapped against him. His broker liquidated the position automatically, and three years of disciplined building, undone by one week of undisciplined defending, was effectively gone.

The thing I think about most with Cooper is that he was not a stupid man, and he was not undisciplined anywhere else in his life. If you had asked him, in the abstract, on a calm afternoon, "should a trader ever move a stop away from price to avoid being filled," he would have looked at you like *you* were the slow one. *Of course not. That violates every principle there is.* And then, in the heat of a real trade, with real money and a real story playing out in his real head, he did it anyway. He did it because the abstract principle and the in-the-moment temptation are two different things, tested by two different versions of the same man.

Now I want you to see something that should make the hair on your arm stand up.

Cooper was running, on a five-figure account in a spare bedroom, the exact program that once took down a bank that had stood for two hundred and thirty-three years.

In 1995, a young trader named Nick Leeson sat on the Singapore futures desk of Barings, a London merchant bank founded in 1762, old enough to have helped finance the Napoleonic Wars. Leeson took positions in Nikkei 225 futures that went against him. He could not take the loss. So he did what Cooper did and what Marcus is, at this very moment, being tempted to do. He made the position bigger to lower his breakeven. Then bigger. He hid the losses in a quiet error account. He kept doubling, the way a man at a roulette table doubles after every red, convinced that the math owes him a black. The market did not care that the math felt owed. By the time it was over, the losses ran past eight hundred million pounds, the bank that had survived two centuries was sold for one pound, and Leeson was in a Singapore prison.

A retail account in a spare bedroom and a 233-year-old bank, brought down by the identical disease. Not a strategy disease. Not an analysis disease. The disease of a human being who could not, in the moment, accept a small certain loss, and so accepted, instead, an enormous uncertain one.

In *Trade Calm*, the companion to this book, that voice has names. The part that refuses to close a loser because of how much is already sunk into it, we call the Sunk-Coster. The part that believes a run of losses is owed a win, we call the Gambler. You do not need the full roster of twelve here. You need to know three things about that voice: it is older than you, it is not on your side, and it has bankrupted people far more sophisticated than you or me. Where it lives in the nervous system, and how to put it on a leash, is a whole book of its own. It is the other book. In *this* book, we do something simpler and just as powerful. We build a structure that does not require you to win the argument with the voice at all.

Two Versions of You

Here is the hinge of everything, so I am going to slow down and say it plainly.

The version of Marcus who set that stop at $69.85, calm, an hour ago, coffee still hot, is not the same creature as the version with his finger on the mouse at 11:47. They share a name and a body. They do not share a nervous system.

Trade Calm calls them the Professor and the Lizard. The Professor is the slow, deliberate, rule-writing mind, the one that reads the chapter, runs the math, and decides, sensibly, where the trade is wrong. The Lizard is the fast, ancient, survival-first mind that takes the wheel the instant real money is genuinely on the line. The Lizard does not read. The Lizard does not do arithmetic. The Lizard has one job: to make the immediate bad feeling stop. Right now, the immediate bad feeling is the prospect of a realized loss, and the fastest way to make that feeling stop is to cancel the order that would cause it.

You will not out-argue the Lizard in the moment. Nobody does. The entire discipline of risk management is the Professor building, in advance, on a calm afternoon, a structure the Lizard cannot dismantle at 11:47. The stop loss is that structure. So is your position size. So is every rule in this chapter. We are not trying to make you brave in the moment. We are trying to make the moment require no bravery, because the decision was already made by the calmer, smarter version of you, and locked where the Lizard cannot reach it.

That is the whole game. Now let us build it.

Survival Is the Whole Game

Most beginners come to trading believing the goal is to make money.

It is not. The goal is to not run out of money long enough to make money. Those sound like the same goal. They are not, and the difference is the difference between the people who are still here in five years and the people who are not.

Sal, whom you met in the foreword and whom I traded near for years, used to put it in one line. "Kid," he would say, not unkindly, "you are not trying to be right. You are trying to be here."

Think about the casino. The casino has a tiny statistical edge on each game, sometimes two percent, sometimes half. Gamblers, on average, lose. Casinos, on average, are wildly profitable. Why? Not because the edge is large. Because the casino plays enough times for the edge to show up, and it never goes broke in the meantime. It can absorb a hot player, a bad weekend, a cold streak, and keep dealing. As long as it keeps dealing, the tiny edge wins.

You, the trader, are the casino. Your edge, if you build one, will be small. It will look like nothing for weeks at a stretch. The market will hand you runs of losses that have nothing to do with your skill and everything to do with the plain variance of taking risk. Your only job, during those runs, is to still be in business when the variance turns back the other way.

This is the deepest reframe in the book, and almost everyone resists it. The goal is not maximum return. The goal is survival long enough to compound. Internalize that and nearly every other decision gets easier. The trader who risks ten percent of his account per trade has a small but real chance of going broke in any given week. The trader who risks one percent essentially cannot, no matter how unlucky he gets—same strategy, same edge per trade. Only one of them is around in five years to collect on it.

This is also, not by coincidence, exactly what an evaluation measures. A prop firm does not actually care whether you can find a good trade. It cares whether you can survive a bad run without breaching a drawdown line. The daily loss limit, the trailing drawdown, the consistency rule: every one of them is a survival test wearing a strategy costume. The trader who has internalized this chapter walks into an evaluation and finds that its rules describe how he already trades. The trader who has not finds a cage. Dani spent four evaluations discovering which one she was. You can spend none.

You want to be the casino. You want to be here.

The Math That Sets You Free

Every trade is a single sentence with numbers in it: *I will risk X to make Y, with some probability P that I am right.* Strategies, setups, indicators, news, all of it is just input to the X, the Y, and the P. The trade itself is the math.

The math has a name: expectancy, and it is the only number that finally matters:

Expectancy = (Probability of Winning × Average Win)
− (Probability of Losing × Average Loss)

Positive, and trading like this makes money over a large enough sample. Negative, and it loses, no matter how clever your reasoning or how loud your gut. The math does not care about your reasoning.

Here is why that is radical. Most beginners are obsessed with win rate, the percentage of trades that come out green, and they will tell you with pride that they are right seventy percent of the time. That should not impress you, because it says nothing about the *size* of the wins against the size of the losses.

Two traders.

Trader A wins 70% of the time. Her wins are $50. Her losses are $200. Over 100 trades: 70 wins times $50 is $3,500; 30 losses times $200 is $6,000. Net: **negative $2,500.** Right most of the time, losing money.

Trader B wins 40% of the time. His wins are $300. His losses are $100. Over 100 trades: 40 wins times $300 is $12,000; 60 losses times $100 is $6,000. Net: **positive $6,000.** Wrong most of the time, making money.

No trick. No asterisk. Trader B is wrong more often and runs a better business, because his average win is bigger than his average loss by enough to more than pay for the lower hit rate. And here is the part that should worry you: almost everything in your life will conspire to make you Trader A. Your brain wants the hit of being right. You will fight yourself, every day of your career, to stay Trader B. The fight is worth it. There is no other way.

The ratio between what you risk and what you stand to make is the **risk-reward ratio**, and it sets the win rate you need to break even:

Risk-Reward	Break-even Win Rate
1:1	50%
1:1.5	40%
1:2	34%
1:3	25%
1:5	17%

Read that table slowly. At 1:3, you can be wrong three times out of four and still not lose money. That is not a small thing. That is the math standing behind you instead of in front of you, and it is why disciplined traders insist on a minimum ratio before they will take a trade at all. They are not greedy. They are letting the arithmetic do the work that being right cannot reliably do.

Position Sizing: The Hidden Skill

Now the part almost nobody teaches properly, and the single biggest determinant of whether you are still trading in five years. Not your strategy. Not your entries. *How much* you put behind each idea.

The rule, repeated more than any other in this business, with good reason:

> **Never risk more than 1% of your trading capital on a single trade.**

Some push to 2%, some pull back to 0.5%. The number matters less than the principle, which is that no single trade should ever have the power to hurt your account meaningfully.

Watch why, because it is not intuitive. Take a $50,000 account.

Risk **1%** per trade, and a brutal ten-loss streak (which *will* happen if you trade long enough) costs you about 10%. You are at $45,000. It stings. You are fine. You keep going.

Risk **5%** per trade, and the same streak costs you about 40%. You are at $30,000, and to get back to even you now need a 67% gain on what is left. That is much harder than it sounds.

Risk **10%**, and the same streak leaves you near $17,000, needing a 200% return to recover. Most traders never come back from there. They quit, or they reach for a wild revenge trade and finish the job.

This is the asymmetry of drawdowns, and it is cruel and one-directional: a 10% loss needs an 11% gain to recover, a 30% loss needs 43%, a 50% loss needs 100%, a 75% loss needs 300%. You cannot un-lose money easily. The 1% rule is not timidity. It is the math of staying in business.

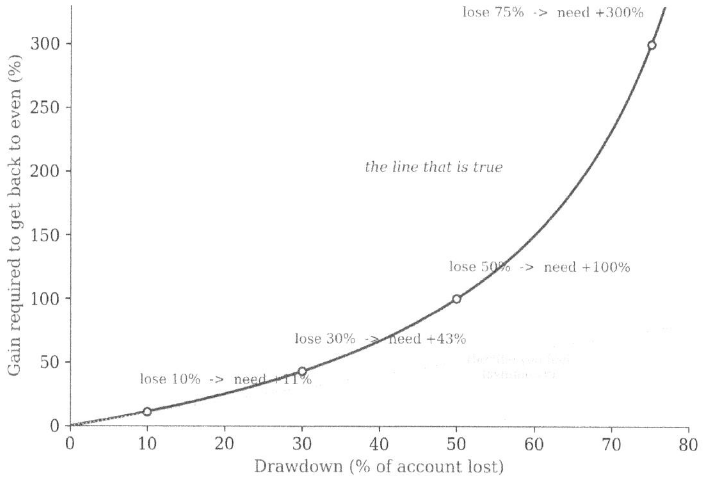

The asymmetry of drawdowns. The gain that undoes a loss is always larger than the loss, and the gap explodes as the hole deepens.

Now make it concrete, because this is where beginners get lost.

- Account: $50,000. Risk budget at 1%: **$500.**
- Trade: long crude oil (CL) at $70.25, stop at $69.85.
- Stop distance: $0.40 a barrel. Crude is 1,000 barrels, so that is **$400 of risk per contract.**
- Position size: $500 ÷ $400 = 1.25 contracts.

You cannot trade a quarter contract, so you size down to **one.** Your real risk is $400, comfortably under budget. Every trade. Every time. You start with the dollars you are allowed to lose, you measure the distance to your stop in the contract's dollars, and you divide. You do not round up because you have a feeling. You do not double down because the setup looks especially good. You size to the math, religiously. And if even one contract blows past your budget, you cannot afford that contract on this account. Trade the Micro version, or skip it. There is no shame in trading the right size for your capital. There is enormous, irreversible shame in trading the wrong size and finding out, halfway down, what that means.

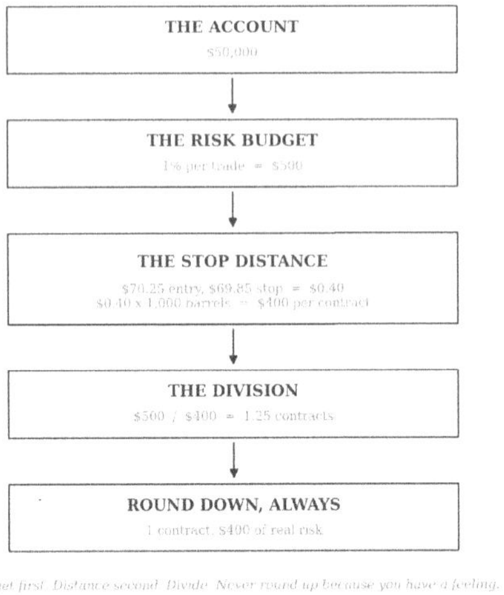

The sizing arithmetic, in the only order that works: budget first, distance second, divide, round down.

The Four Faces of Risk

When people say "risk," they usually mean only the first of four things they should mean.

Market risk is the obvious one. Price moves against you. You manage it with sizing and stops.

Liquidity risk is the risk that when you want out, nobody is there at a fair price, so your stop, when it triggers, slips through empty levels and your planned small loss becomes a large one. It is worst in thin overnight sessions, around holidays, and right after major news. It is why we trade liquid contracts. Dani has met this one personally, in the last chapter.

Leverage risk is the risk that the very thing letting you trade, margin, turns on you. A position gaps past your maintenance margin overnight, the broker liquidates at the worst possible price, and there is no negotiation. This is how traders blow up: not from a slow drift, but from one gap and a forced exit. The defense is the 1% rule, plus never holding more than you could survive if the market gapped hard against you while you slept.

Operational risk is the risk that something breaks. The internet drops mid-trade. The platform crashes on a high-volume day. A power cord gets kicked. These sound like jokes until they happen at the worst possible moment, which is the only moment they happen. The defenses are dull and essential: a reliable platform, your broker's trading-desk phone number saved, and never a position so large you cannot survive losing the ability to manage it.

A good trader respects all four. A great one builds a process for each, in advance, before the trade.

The Religion of the Stop

We have to talk about stops, because the way most traders fail to use them is the single most common cause of accelerated account destruction.

A stop loss is a pre-placed order that closes your position when the price reaches the level at which your idea is wrong. It is not optional. It is not only for beginners. It is the one mechanism that turns your risk discipline from a belief into a fact.

Three sentences. Memorize them. Tape them to the monitor.

> **You enter every trade with the stop already placed. You do not move the stop against you. When it is hit, you take the loss and move on.**

Every trader who has lasted has internalized those three. Every trader who has blown up has, at some point, broken at least one, usually all three. Now the temptations are coming for you.

Trading without a stop. "I will just watch it and get out if it goes against me." This is what every blown-up trader said the first time. The problem is not that you will not be watching. The problem is that the watching brain, with a loss in front of it, will helpfully invent a thousand reasons that this is only noise. Place the stop. Let the stop decide. Remove yourself from the decision in advance.

Moving the stop away from price. This is what got Cooper. This is what got Leeson. This is what is, at this very moment, whispering to Marcus. You set the stop where you set it because, with a clear head, you decided the idea was wrong beyond that level. Moving it does not change the market. It changes your relationship with reality. If the level no longer means the idea is wrong, you were wrong about the level, which means you should not be in the trade. Either way, the honest move is to honor the original stop and get out. Moving it only delays the loss and grows it.

The mental stop. "I do not need a hard order; I will exit when it hits my level." The trouble is that the same mind meant to enforce it is the mind currently clouded by the discomfort of the open loss. You cannot ask the most compromised part of your brain to be the part that pulls the trigger. The hard order goes into the market. The market enforces it. You are not given the chance to reconsider.

There is exactly one direction it is acceptable to move a stop after entry, and that is *in your favor*. As a trade moves into profit, trailing the stop up behind it, locking in gains and bleeding off risk, is professional practice. Stops move in your favor, never against you. Ever.

The Trades That Pay for the Other Ones

Now look briefly at the upside, because the discipline above exists to make room for it.

A great trade is not merely one with a decent ratio. It is *asymmetric*, where the reward, if you are right, is many times the risk you took. The legendary fortunes were built on a handful of these. Soros breaking the pound in 1992 was an asymmetric bet, a contained risk against an enormous potential return. The traders who shorted the housing market in 2008 paid small premiums for gigantic payouts. You will almost certainly never place a Soros trade. But once a month, once a quarter, you will see a setup where everything lines up: the structure, the catalyst, the level, the time of day, and those are the trades you scale up *within your risk limits*, and those are the ones that, over years, turn a modest account into a meaningful one. Wait for them. Recognize them. Take them.

The Quiet Math That Funds You

Let me end the teaching on a more hopeful note, because everything so far has been warnings, and you have earned a look at what discipline buys.

Take a $25,000 account and a competent trader earning 1.5% a month after costs. Not glamorous. Not a YouTube number. Roughly what a decent professional actually compounds, and most months you will not even hit it.

- After one year: **$29,890.** Better than the index.
- After three years: **$42,728.** Nearly doubled.
- After five years: **$61,080.**
- After ten years: **$149,233.** Six times the start.
- After twenty years: **$890,820.** Financially independent, from a $25,000 stake and modest skill.

That is what compounding does, and it is why survival matters so much. You do not need a 30% month. You do not need a viral system. You need to be *not broke* for long enough that the slow miracle has time to work. The trader who risks small and compounds modestly beats the trader who risks big and gets famous, almost every time. It is also, for the trader without much capital, the entire case for getting funded: a small edge run on a firm's larger account, survived and repeated, is how modest skill turns into a real income years sooner than it could on a spare-bedroom stake. But only if you can hold the line long enough to be trusted with the size. The firm is just the casino, checking whether you are a gambler before it lets you deal.

That, in the end, is the funded edge. Not a secret, not a hidden indicator. The willingness to be patient with risk, religious about stops, and humble about size, for long enough that the math does its slow work on your behalf. It is what passes the evaluation. It is what survives the first payout. Most people cannot do it. Their egos demand faster proof. You do not have to be one of them.

Back to Marcus

So. Marcus, 11:47, finger on the mouse, ten cents from his stop, the reasonable voice in his ear. What did he do?

He moved the stop. Of course he did. Almost everyone does, the first time. He slid it down to $69.60, to give it room, just this once. The price touched $69.62, hung there long enough to make him feel like a genius, and then kept going. He moved it again. By the time he finally hit the market sell in something close to panic, the trade that should have cost him $400 had cost him a little over $1,400. He sat looking at a number that was not, in the scheme of an account, fatal, but was three and a half times the loss he had agreed to take an hour earlier when he was still himself.

Here is the part that matters, and the reason Marcus is going to keep showing up in this book. That night, he did the one thing that turns a loss into an education instead of a wound. He wrote it down. The setup, the entry, the stop he set, the stop he moved, and, in plain language, the sentence that is the whole of it: *I knew the rule, and I broke it anyway, because the loss felt avoidable and I wanted it to be.* He showed it to Sal a week later. Sal read it, slid it back across the table, and said, "Good. Now you have met him. The trick is not to never meet him again. The trick is to build the thing he cannot touch."

The thing he cannot touch is everything in this chapter. The stop placed before entry, where the calm Professor can reach it but the panicking Lizard cannot. The position size that makes one bad trade survivable. The 1% that makes a ten-loss streak a bad month instead of a closed account. None of it requires you to win the argument at 11:47. All of it requires you to have already won it, hours earlier, when you were reasonable, and then to have locked the conclusion somewhere your unreasonable self cannot get to.

Whether you can *do* that, consistently, over years, when the voice is good, and the loss feels avoidable, and your finger is on the mouse, is not finally a question of structure. It is a question of the mind that operates the structure. That question, the whole of it, is what *Trade Calm* is for. This book makes you literate in the market and keeps you alive in it. That one teaches you to be the person who can hold the line. Read this one first. You will know when you are ready for the other.

For now, settle in. We have spent four chapters on the deepest principles. You know what trading is, who is on the other side, how the plumbing works, and what risk really means. In the next chapter we get concrete, into the contract itself, the fine print that, ignored, has bankrupted otherwise excellent traders.

It is, in some ways, the most boring chapter in the book. It is also the one you will reach for most in your first year.

CHAPTER 4, KEY IDEAS

- **Survival is the whole game.** The goal is not maximum return; it is staying in business long enough for a small edge to compound. Be the casino, not the gambler. Every evaluation rule is a survival test in disguise.
- **There are two of you**—the calm Professor who plans the trade and the panicking Lizard who runs it once money is live. Risk management is the Professor building, in advance, a structure the Lizard cannot dismantle.
- **The same disease scales.** Cooper could not take a small loss and lost an account. Nick Leeson could not take a small loss and lost a 233-year-old bank. The Sunk-Coster and the Gambler do not care about the size of the account.
- **Risk and reward are one thing.** Every trade is *risk X to make Y at probability P*. Expectancy is the only number that finally matters, and a high win rate without a good ratio is a slow way to lose.
- **The 1% rule is non-negotiable.** No single trade should be able to hurt your account. Size from the stop distance, every time, and round down.
- **Drawdowns are asymmetric.** A 50% loss needs a 100% gain to recover. Do not dig holes you cannot climb out of.
- **The stop is a vow, not a guess.** Placed before entry, never moved against you, honored when hit. Moving it is the exact move that took down Cooper, Leeson, and nearly Marcus.
- **The funded edge is quiet.** Modest returns, survived and repeated, are what pass an evaluation, hold a funded account, and compound into real money. The discipline to hold the line while the Lizard screams is the greatest skill there is, and it is the subject of *Trade Calm*.

CHAPTER 5

The Anatomy of a Contract

The number that finally got Marcus's attention was one thousand.

He had been trading crude oil for two weeks before he truly understood that one contract was a thousand barrels, and that when the price moved a single dollar, from $70 to $71, his one little contract gained or lost a thousand dollars. Not a dollar. Not seventy. A thousand. He had been clicking buy on a quarter of a quarter-million dollars of oil as casually as buying a coffee, because the screen only ever showed him "1," and "1" felt small. Sal put it to him over the phone in his gravel voice. "You keep saying you bought one. One what. You bought a promise to take delivery of a thousand barrels of oil. You got somewhere to put a thousand barrels of oil, Marcus."

A futures contract is a strange object to look at the first time. Most beginners assume it is something like a stock, a thing you own that has a price and goes up and down. It is not. It is a promise, and it has more in common with a marriage license than with a share of Apple.

This chapter is what is actually inside the promise. The specifications, the obligations, the timing, the math of how money moves between accounts when the price changes, and the question of what happens if you are still holding the thing when it expires. By the end, you should be able to look at any futures contract on any screen and answer, instantly, the three questions every trader has to answer before placing the trade. What am I actually agreeing to? How much am I actually risking with one contract? What happens to me if I am still holding this when it expires?

These sound trivial. They are not. The reason most retail traders make catastrophic mistakes in their first year is not bad strategy. It is failing to understand, in the moment, exactly what their contract represents and exactly how much money is in motion on each tick. Marcus nearly learned it the expensive way. We are going to fix it the cheap way, here, permanently.

What a Contract Actually Is

Strip away the technology, the platforms, the screens, the algorithms, and a futures contract is this:

> A standardized, legally binding agreement, traded on a regulated exchange, in which one party promises to buy and another promises to sell a specific quantity of a specific underlying asset at a specific price on a specific future date.

Six phrases are doing all the work. Pull each apart.

Standardized. Every futures contract for a given product is identical to every other for that product. You do not negotiate the terms of an individual contract; the exchange has already defined them. This is what separates futures from the older, looser instrument called a forward contract, which is custom-negotiated between two parties and trades only between them. Standardization is the magic that lets millions of strangers trade with each other without knowing or trusting each other. The contract is interchangeable, fungible, anonymous.

Legally binding. This is not a wager between friends. It is a contract, with the full weight of contract law and exchange-rule enforcement behind it. Go long a December crude oil contract and hold it through expiration, and you have legally agreed to take delivery of a thousand barrels of crude at the price you contracted for. The oil is real. The obligation is real. Most retail traders never face it because they close before expiration, but it is there in the background, and you should respect it. Marcus, two weeks in, did not know it was there.

Traded on a regulated exchange. Futures do not trade peer-to-peer. They trade on centralized exchanges, the CME Group in Chicago, ICE Futures, Eurex in Frankfurt, that match buyers with sellers and guarantee the trades through a clearinghouse. The clearinghouse is the unsung hero of the system. When you buy a contract, you are not really buying from a specific seller; you are buying from the clearinghouse, which has bought from the seller. It stands in the middle of every trade, guarantees performance on both sides, and collects margin from everyone to make sure it can. This is why you never worry about counterparty risk in futures. The clearinghouse handles it.

Specific quantity of a specific underlying asset. The contract specifies, in writing, exactly what one contract represents. One crude oil contract (CL) is 1,000 barrels, the number that got Marcus. One gold contract (GC) is 100 troy ounces. One E-mini S&P 500 contract (ES) is $50 times the index. One corn contract (ZC) is 5,000 bushels. The exchange decides these sizes. You do not.

Specific price. The price at which you agreed to transact. This is the only thing actually being negotiated in the moment. Everything else- the size, the asset, the date- is fixed in advance. The only variable is the price at which you and another party are willing to meet.

Specific future date. The expiration. Every futures contract has one, after which it ceases to exist as a tradeable instrument and becomes either a delivery obligation, for physically settled contracts, or a cash payment, for cash-settled ones. The contract is finite by design. This is one of the most important differences between futures and stocks, and it shapes everything about how you trade them.

The Specification Sheet: Your Owner's Manual

Every futures contract has a publicly available specification sheet, the spec sheet, that lists in cold detail every property of the contract you are about to trade. You should read it. You should actually read it. Not skim it, not assume you know what it says. Open the spec sheet for any contract before your first trade in it and confirm, with your own eyes, the contract size, the quote unit, the tick size, the tick value, the trading hours including the overnight session, the expiration and contract months, the settlement type, the first notice day, the last trading day, the daily price limits, and the initial and maintenance margin.

Every one of these matters. Skip one and at some point in your career it will hurt you. Let me walk through the ones most likely to.

Contract Size: How Big Is One?

The single most misunderstood part of futures trading among beginners is the size of one contract. People look at a quote, crude oil at $70, and naturally assume buying one contract costs $70. It does not. Buying one contract of crude costs nothing up front; you only post margin. But the contract represents $70 times 1,000 barrels, which is $70,000 of crude oil exposure.

When crude moves from $70 to $71, a one-dollar move, your contract gains or loses $1,000. Not one dollar. Not seventy. One thousand, per contract. This is the leverage we met in Chapter 1. You posted maybe $5,000 in margin to control $70,000 of oil. The contract behaves as though you own the whole $70,000. A 1.4% move is roughly $1,000, about a 20% swing on your posted margin, in either direction. The contract is hyper-responsive to price, and the responsiveness is what makes it both attractive and dangerous.

Here are the contract sizes for the most-traded contracts. Commit the ones you trade to memory, because this table will save you from arithmetic disasters.

Symbol	Contract	One Contract Represents
ES	E-mini S&P 500	$50 x index (about $250k)
MES	Micro E-mini S&P 500	$5 x index (about $25k)
NQ	E-mini Nasdaq 100	$20 x index (about $400k)
MNQ	Micro E-mini Nasdaq 100	$2 x index (about $40k)
CL	Crude Oil (WTI)	1,000 barrels (about $70k)
MCL	Micro Crude Oil	100 barrels (about $7k)
GC	Gold	100 troy ounces (about $240k)
MGC	Micro Gold	10 troy ounces (about $24k)
ZN	10-Year Treasury Note	$100,000 face value
6E	Euro FX	125,000 euro (about $135k)
ZW	Wheat	5,000 bushels (about $30k)
NG	Natural Gas	10,000 MMBtu (about $25k)

(Approximate notional values at reference levels of index 5,000 for the S&P, 20,000 for the Nasdaq, crude at $70, gold at $2,400, wheat at $6, natural gas at $2.50, and the euro at 1.08. All are illustrative and move with the market.)

Two things to notice. First, the standard contracts are enormous in notional value. A single E-mini S&P contract controls a quarter million dollars of equity exposure. A single gold contract controls nearly a quarter million dollars of gold. These numbers should give you pause every time you click buy. They are exactly what Sal was trying to make Marcus feel.

Second, there are micro contracts for almost every major product now, one-tenth the size of the standard. They were introduced precisely so smaller accounts could trade with proper risk control, and they are the reason the small-account trader and the prop-firm hopeful can exist at all. If you have less than about $50,000 to trade with, you should be using micros, full stop. The standard contracts produce too much dollar variance per tick for a small account to handle inside the 1% rule we built in the last chapter. This is where that rule gets concrete. It is also, quietly, the on-ramp the whole funded movement runs on: a trader with a few thousand dollars can practice real risk discipline on micros until a firm is willing to rent her the size she cannot fund herself. Dani built her whole method on the micro E-mini before she ever bought an evaluation.

Tick Size and Tick Value: The Currency of Your P&L

A tick is the smallest price change allowed for a contract. The exchange defines it. You do not trade at prices between ticks; it is the minimum granularity. The E-mini S&P has a tick size of 0.25 index points. Price can move from 4,832.00 to 4,832.25 to 4,832.50, but not to 4,832.10 or 4,832.37. This matters because it constrains how you set entries, stops, and targets. They all have to sit at tick-aligned levels.

A tick value is the dollar amount of one tick. This is the number you actually feel in your P&L. For the E-mini S&P, tick size 0.25 points times the $50 multiplier is $12.50 per contract. For crude, $0.01 per barrel times 1,000 barrels is $10. For gold, $0.10 per ounce times 100 ounces is $10.

Contract	Tick Size	Tick Value
ES	0.25 points	$12.50
MES	0.25 points	$1.25
NQ	0.25 points	$5.00

Contract	Tick Size	Tick Value
MNQ	0.25 points	$0.50
CL	$0.01 / bbl	$10.00
MCL	$0.01 / bbl	$1.00
GC	$0.10 / oz	$10.00
MGC	$0.10 / oz	$1.00
ZN	1/64 of a point	$15.625
6E	$0.00005 / euro	$6.25

Why does this matter in practice? Because every risk and reward calculation you make is in ticks, every tick has a dollar value, and you cannot afford to get the conversion wrong. Look at a crude setup: buy $70.25, stop $69.85. That is 40 cents of risk, or 40 ticks. At $10 a tick, dollar risk per contract is $400. For a $50,000 account at 1% risk, you can trade $500 divided by $400, which is 1.25 contracts, so one contract. (You will recognize that trade. It is the one Marcus was sitting in at 11:47 in the last chapter, before he moved the stop he had so carefully calculated.)

The arithmetic is trivial when you do it slowly. It goes invisible when you do it fast under pressure, and one transposed digit can cost you everything. Always compute risk in ticks first, multiply by tick value for dollar risk, divide your dollar budget by per-contract dollar risk for position size. Working through those four steps in that order, every single trade, is part of what separates traders who survive from traders who think they are better at mental math than they are.

Margin: Performance Bond, Not a Loan

We touched margin in Chapter 1. Now deeper, because the difference between futures margin and stock margin is the kind of confusion that destroys accounts.

When you buy stock on margin, your broker is lending you money. You put up half the price, the broker fronts the other half, you pay interest on the loan, and you own the stock. The margin is debt.

When you trade futures on margin, your broker is not lending you anything. There is no loan, no interest. You are not buying anything; you are promising to buy something later, and the broker is collecting a good-faith deposit, a security deposit, to make sure you can keep your promise if the price moves against you. The technical name is the performance bond.

This is subtle but critical. In stock margin, the money you posted is part of your purchase. In futures margin, the money you posted is separate from the contract. It is collateral held by the clearinghouse to guarantee your performance. If the contract gains value, money flows into your account from the other side of the trade. If it loses, money flows out. The margin is the buffer that ensures you can fund the flows out without defaulting.

Three levels of margin to know. Initial margin is what you must post to open a position. The exchange sets it; your broker may require slightly more, and it moves up or down with volatility, rising when markets get wild so participants can cover potential losses. As a rough rule, it runs 3% to 10% of notional. For the E-mini S&P in normal conditions, initial margin is around $13,000 per contract on roughly $250,000 of exposure, about 5%. For crude, often around $5,000 on $70,000, about 7%. Treat these dollar figures as a snapshot, not a quote. The exchange resets margins with volatility, sometimes overnight, so check the current requirement before you trade.

Maintenance margin is the minimum balance you must keep to hold the position open, typically around 90% of the initial. If your account equity, your cash plus the mark-to-market value of your open position, drops below maintenance, you get a margin call, a demand to deposit funds to bring the account back to the initial level. If you do not meet it quickly, and quickly can mean within hours, your broker will liquidate your position at the prevailing price. They will not call to discuss it. They will not extend the benefit of the doubt. They will close the trade, take whatever the market gives, and book the loss. This is how leveraged traders blow up. Not from a slow decline they manage carefully, but from a single move that drops them through the maintenance threshold and triggers an automated, indifferent liquidation. It is the same machinery that finished Cooper's overnight position in the last chapter. And it is the private-account cousin of the rule that ends most evaluations: a prop firm's trailing drawdown is just a maintenance threshold with a friendlier name, an automated line that closes you out the instant your equity touches it, no negotiation, no benefit of the doubt. Learn to respect the broker's line, and you will already understand the firm's.

Variation margin, or mark-to-market settlement, is what happens every day in every futures account at the end of every session. The clearinghouse marks every position to the closing price. Profits are credited to winning accounts, losses debited from losing ones. The cash moves every day. Hold a winner today, and your cash balance rose by what you won. Hold a loser, and it fell by what you lost. This is daily settlement, one of the deep structural features that makes futures safer for the system as a whole, because losses are not allowed to pile up silently as unrealized paper. They are recognized and funded every day. What it means for you: you cannot ignore a losing position for a week and hope it recovers, because every day the loss is debited from your cash. Eventually you run out, or breach maintenance, and the position is closed for you. Futures do not let you pretend.

Leverage: The Multiplier and the Cliff

Let me make leverage explicit, because the abstract idea is easy to wave at and hard to feel until the numbers are laid out. Take one E-mini S&P contract at index 5,000. Notional value, $50 times 5,000, is $250,000. Initial margin, about $13,000. Leverage ratio, roughly 19 to 1.

A 1% move in the index moves the notional 1%, which is $2,500, a gain or loss against the $13,000 you posted. In other words, a 1% move in the index produces a 19% move in your margin equity.

This is the leverage cliff, and it is steeper than people who have not traded futures realize. On a perfectly ordinary day, a 1.5% decline that happens several times a year on no dramatic news produces a $3,750 loss on a single contract. If you posted only $13,000, you are down 29% on the trade in one session. If you posted the bare minimum and the market moves 2.5% against you, routine in volatile stretches, you have blown through your entire posted margin and your broker is calling for more.

The leverage cuts both ways, of course. The same 1% in your favor is a 19% gain. This is the seduction. It is why people walk into futures expecting to get rich quickly. They are not wrong about the upside.

They are wrong about how much downside is required to play that game.

The defense against the cliff is the one we built in Chapter 4. Position sizing. The 1% rule, calculated from your stop distance, ensures even a worst-case adverse move on your largest position does not threaten your account. The leverage is real, but it is bounded by the size of the position you choose. One contract on a $250,000 account is barely leveraged in account terms. One contract on a $25,000 account is dangerously leveraged. Same contract, different account, different exposure. This is the answer to the question every new trader silently asks: how many contracts should I trade? Not as many as the margin allows. The margin requirement is the minimum, set by the exchange, with no regard for your survival. Your own risk discipline sets your position size. Always size from your stop and your account, never from the margin minimum.

Settlement: How the Contract Ends

Every futures contract eventually expires, and when it does, one of two things happens. Physical delivery or cash settlement.

Physical delivery means what it sounds like. The underlying commodity actually changes hands. Whoever held the long at expiration is obligated to take delivery. Whoever held the short is obligated to deliver. The exchange manages the logistics, the delivery locations, the grade certification, the warehouse receipts, but the obligation is real. The physically delivered contracts include most physical commodities: crude oil, natural gas, gold, silver, copper, wheat, corn, soybeans, live cattle, coffee, sugar, cotton. Hold one through expiration as a speculator with no warehouse, no truck, no facility to receive a thousand barrels of oil or 5,000 bushels of corn, and you have a real, embarrassing, expensive problem, because the exchange does not care that you did not mean to. This is the cliff Marcus could not see, standing in his spare bedroom thinking he had bought "one."

In practice, fewer than 3% of futures contracts ever result in actual delivery. The other 97% are closed before expiration by speculators who roll forward into the next contract month or exit. You will be doing the same. But you have to know the deadlines, because the obligation kicks in earlier than the formal expiration. The critical deadline for physically settled contracts is First Notice Day, the first day the exchange can assign delivery obligations to longs. Hold a long on or after First Notice Day, and you can be served a delivery notice, even though the contract technically hasn't expired yet. The window between First Notice Day and Last Trading Day is the danger zone. You want to be out before First Notice Day, period. A simple rule: for physically delivered contracts, exit or roll at least one full week before First Notice Day, and you will never have an unwanted delivery. Your platform usually shows the dates. Pay attention.

Cash settlement is much simpler. When a cash-settled contract expires, the exchange calculates a final settlement price: for the index futures, a special opening quotation built from the index's opening prices on expiration morning, for others an average over a defined window, and all open positions close at that price. Cash moves to reflect the final P&L, and the contract ceases to exist. No commodity, no delivery, no logistics, only money. The cash-settled contracts include all the stock index futures (ES, NQ, RTY, YM), the volatility futures (VX), and the SOFR interest-rate futures. The major currency futures, including the Euro FX from the tables above, are technically deliverable, so treat them like the physical contracts and exit or roll before expiration. The index and rate contracts are the speculator-friendly ones. You can hold them to expiration, and the worst thing that happens is they auto-close at the final price: no delivery anxiety, no First Notice Day to track. For most retail speculators, this is one of several reasons to weight your trading toward the major index futures, and it is no accident that the index futures are also what nearly every prop evaluation is traded on. Cash settlement removes an entire category of operational risk from your life. You still mind the calendar; you do not want to be long a contract about to expire while the new month is already trading more actively, but the catastrophic-mistake potential of physical delivery is not there.

The Contract Calendar: Front Month, Back Month, and the Roll

One last operational detail beginners stumble over. Futures are listed in monthly cycles. For any product, there are multiple contracts available at once, each expiring in a different month. Crude has contracts for essentially every month for years out. The E-mini S&P has quarterly expirations: March, June, September, December, several quarters out.

At any moment, though, almost all the volume is concentrated in a single month, the one closest to expiration but not yet inside its delivery window. This is the front month, also called the front contract or active month. The contracts further out are the back months, with lower volume, wider spreads, and worse liquidity. As a rule, you trade the front month. You do not trade the back months unless you have a specific reason and understand what you are giving up in liquidity.

As the front month approaches expiration, two things happen at once. Volume in the front month starts to fall, and volume in the next month starts to rise. There is a brief window, usually about a week, when both are heavily traded as the market transitions. This is the roll period, and traders holding positions through it must roll, closing the expiring contract and simultaneously opening an equivalent position in the new front month. If you close intraday or within a few days, you may never think about the roll; your trades complete inside one contract month. Hold for weeks or longer, and you will roll periodically. Most platforms make it easy: a spread order that closes the old and opens the new with one click. Pay the small spread cost, accept the tiny gain or loss from the price difference between months, and move on.

What matters most: know which contract you are actually trading. Most platforms default to the front month, but you can place an order in a back month if you are not paying attention, and back months are illiquid enough that you will pay dearly for it. Look at the contract month every single time. Three keystrokes. Worth it.

Putting It All Together: Reading a Trade in Full

Let me close with a worked example that pulls everything together. This is the mental walk-through you should do every single time before placing a trade, and it is, not coincidentally, exactly the discipline an evaluation is built to verify you have.

You are looking at the December E-mini S&P 500, symbol ESZ, on a Tuesday morning, and assume for this example that it is the active front month at the time you take the trade. The price is 4,832.25. You believe the price is going up and you want to go long. (*The active month depends on the calendar; confirm the current front contract before trading.*)

Step one: confirm the contract. ESZ, December. Cash settled. The front month for this example. Standard size, $50 multiplier, tick size 0.25 points, tick value $12.50.

Step two, identify your stop. Your analysis says the trade is invalidated below 4,825.00. That is your stop.

Step three, compute dollar risk per contract. Distance, 4,832.25 minus 4,825.00, is 7.25 points. In ticks, 7.25 divided by 0.25 is 29 ticks. Dollar risk per contract, 29 times $12.50, is $362.50.

Step four, identify your target. Your analysis puts a reasonable objective at 4,855.00. Distance, 22.75 points, is 91 ticks, or $1,137.50 per contract.

Step five, check the risk-reward. $362.50 risk against $1,137.50 reward is 1 to 3.14. Good ratio. Mathematically attractive.

Step six: position size from your account. Account $50,000. 1% risk, $500. Maximum contracts, $500 divided by $362.50, about 1.38. Round down to one contract.

Step seven, confirm margin. Initial margin per contract, about $13,000 against a $50,000 account, is 26% of the account in margin. Acceptable, with plenty of buffer for variation margin if the trade moves against you intraday.

Step eight, place the trade. Buy one ESZ at market, or with a limit at 4,832.25 if you can wait. Immediately place a stop-loss to sell one at 4,825.00. Immediately place a profit-target limit to sell one at 4,855.00. Use a bracket order if your platform supports it, so all three go in together.

Step nine, walk away. Or watch, if you must, but you have no more decisions to make. The trade resolves at the stop or the target. If at any point you find yourself wanting to move the stop further from price, re-read Chapter 4. If you find yourself wanting to add because it is going your way, you may do so only if you have a documented rule for adding that you decided before entering. Otherwise, you let it run.

That is what a properly structured trade looks like. Every step deliberate. Every number computed. No moves made under pressure. The structure protects you from yourself, which, if you remember Marcus at 11:47, is the only protection that reliably holds.

This is what we mean in this book by a professional trader. Not the title. Not the income. The process. The thing that separates trading from gambling is not the size of the bets. Gamblers bet large and traders bet small, but that is not it either. It is the structure around each bet, and whether that structure is in place before the money goes on the line. That, more than any other skill, is what this book is trying to teach, and it is the visible half of a deeper discipline whose other half, the mind that honors the structure when every nerve says to abandon it, is the work of *Trade Calm*.

In the next chapter we leave the mechanics behind and move into the first of the truly analytical skills: how to look at a market and form a hypothesis about where price is going. Welcome to market analysis.

CHAPTER 5, KEY IDEAS

- **A futures contract is a standardized, legally binding promise** to exchange a specific quantity of a specific asset at a specific price on a specific date. The standardization is what makes the market possible.
- **The clearinghouse stands in the middle of every trade.** You carry no counterparty risk against the person on the other side, only against the clearinghouse, which is engineered to be unbreakable.
- **Contract size is enormous.** A single E-mini S&P contract controls about $250,000 of exposure, and one crude contract is a thousand barrels. Use micro contracts, one-tenth the size, for accounts under $50,000. Micros are the on-ramp the whole funded movement runs on.
- **Tick, times tick value, times stop distance, equals dollar risk.** Compute it every time, then divide your 1% budget by it for position size, and round down. Do not skip it.

- **Futures margin is a performance bond, not a loan.** No interest, no ownership, just collateral held by the clearinghouse to guarantee you can meet daily mark-to-market. A prop firm's trailing drawdown is the same idea with a friendlier name.
- **Mark-to-market settlement happens daily.** Losses are debited from your cash every day. You cannot ignore a losing position. The market does not allow it.
- **Physical delivery versus cash settlement matters.** Exit physically delivered contracts well before First Notice Day. Cash-settled index futures can be held to expiration without delivery risk, which is why nearly every evaluation is traded on them.
- **Trade the front month.** Volume, liquidity, and tight spreads live there. Back months are for specialists. Look at the contract month every time.
- **Walk every trade through the nine steps:** confirm contract, stop level, dollar risk, target, risk-reward, position size, margin check, place with bracket, walk away. Religious practice. Every time. It is also exactly what an evaluation is checking for.

CHAPTER 6

Reading the Tea Leaves

By his third week, Marcus had discovered indicators, and he had discovered them the way a teenager discovers cologne—all at once and far too much of it.

His chart had nine of them stacked on it. Two moving averages, a thing with three colored bands, an oscillator that swung between zero and a hundred, and a few he could not have explained if you held his account hostage. He sent Sal a screenshot, a little proud of it, and Sal wrote back a single sentence that Marcus would remember for years. "You have put nine pairs of sunglasses on, and now you are wondering why it is dark."

Then Sal said the thing this chapter is about. "Take them all off. Learn to read the price first. The price is the only thing in the picture that is actually true." A few days later he sent Marcus a single bare chart, no indicators, and read it back to him three different ways depending on which timeframe he stood on, the same forty bars a downtrend up close, a pullback inside an uptrend from farther back, and noise from farther still. "Same chart," Sal wrote. "Three honest stories. The skill is knowing which one you are trading."

There is a famous division in market analysis, and it is the source of more pointless arguments than almost any other topic in finance. On one side are the fundamentalists, who believe markets must, in the end, obey the underlying economic reality. The price of crude reflects supply and demand for crude. The price of the S&P 500 reflects the aggregate earnings power of five hundred American corporations. To know where a market is going, the fundamentalist says, you must understand the real-world drivers: inventories, earnings, growth, rate differentials, geopolitics. Charts are decorative. Fundamentals are real.

On the other side are the technicians, who believe all the relevant information is already in the price, that the chart itself is the most reliable source available, and that the behavior of price, its trends, its patterns, its reactions at specific levels, encodes everything you need to trade it. The technician will tell you, with some justification, that they have made money in markets they did not understand fundamentally and lost money in markets they understood thoroughly. Fundamentals are noise. The chart is real.

Each camp produces books, gurus, conferences, podcasts, and a steady supply of converts convinced the other camp is composed of imbeciles. The argument has run for about a hundred years and shows no sign of ending, mostly because both sides are partly right.

Here is the honest version, with the slow build-up spared. Fundamentals tell you where prices should go eventually. Technicals tell you where prices are going now. And "eventually" and "now" are very different timescales when you are holding a leveraged position. You can be completely right about the fundamentals and still be wiped out by the technicals before you collect, because the market does not care what is supposed to happen until the participants collectively decide to care, and that can take days, weeks, or years. The graveyard is full of traders who were right too early, which in this business is the same as being wrong. Dani has a headstone in that graveyard. Her first evaluation died on a trade she was eventually proven right about, a week after the trailing drawdown had already closed her account. Being right later is not a category an evaluation recognizes.

For our purposes, short-to-medium-term leveraged futures trading, the technical side does most of the heavy lifting. We use fundamentals to set our broad orientation: am I biased long, short, or neutral on this market over the next month, and we use technicals to time entries and exits. We will not become pure technicians who refuse to read the news, nor pure fundamentalists who place trades on a thesis without ever looking at the chart. We will become traders who understand both lenses, know what each is good for, and never confuse one for the other.

This chapter is the foundation of the technical side. It is about the irreducible skill of looking at a price chart and reading it and not interpreting it, not predicting it. Reading what it is telling you, the way a doctor reads an X-ray. The information is right there. You have to learn to see it. And you see it better, as Sal told Marcus, with the nine pairs of sunglasses off.

The Chart Is Not a Crystal Ball

Before we go further, let me dispense with the most damaging myth in technical analysis, that the chart predicts the future.

It does not. It cannot. No chart, no pattern, no indicator, no system has ever predicted anything, and none could in principle, because the future depends on the next thing that happens, the next news event, the next number, the next surprise, and the chart contains zero information about events that have not occurred.

What the chart does tell you is what has already happened, what the current state of supply and demand looks like, and what similar setups have tended to produce in the past. From that you construct probabilities. Informed estimates of the direction a market is more likely to move next, and the levels where it is more likely to find friction: probabilities, not predictions. The difference is everything.

A technician does not say "the market is going up." A technician says: based on the structure of price action over the past several weeks, the conditions that historically precede an upward move are present. I will take a long with a defined stop, sized appropriately, and let the trade resolve. Wrong, I lose a little. Right, I make more. The expectancy is positive. That is the entire intellectual stance of technical analysis: probabilities, asymmetric outcomes, defined risk. Anyone telling you they know what the market is about to do is selling something. Politely refuse.

The Atom of the Chart: One Price Bar

Start at the lowest resolution—the single price bar.

A price bar, also called a candlestick in the more common candle format, is a compressed summary of what happened to price during a defined period. One minute, five minutes, an hour, a day, a week-your choice, depending on your time horizon. Whatever the period, the bar always carries the same four numbers: the open, the first price traded in the period. The high, the highest reached. The low, the lowest. The close, the last price traded. These four, OHLC in the shorthand, encode into a visual mark you can read at a glance.

In a candlestick chart, the body spans the distance between open and close. It is colored green or white if the close was higher than the open, red or black if lower. The wicks, sometimes called shadows, are the thin lines above and below the body, marking the high and the low.

That sounds trivial. It is not. A single well-formed candle tells you four useful things at once: the net direction during the period, shown by color; the size of the move, the length of the body; the range, top of the upper wick to bottom of the lower; and the location of the close within the range, where the body sits relative to the wicks. Combine those four, and you start to see structure where beginners see noise. A big green body with tiny wicks says buyers dominated the period: price opened, went almost straight up, closed near the high. A big red body with a long lower wick says sellers dominated early, drove price down, then buyers stepped in and pushed it back. The close was still down, but the story is "sellers tried, buyers fought back, unresolved." Those two candles look completely different even though both are negative, and they imply different things about what comes next.

Beginners ignore wicks. Professionals stare at them. Wicks are where the interesting information lives. A long wick means the market tested that level, went there, and then rejected it, and the rejection is meaningful. It tells you that at some price during the period, enough opposing pressure showed up to drive price back. Wicks are footprints of fights you did not see.

There are whole schools built around candle shapes, bullish engulfings, dragonfly dojis, hanging men, three white soldiers, evening stars. Most of the names are colorful, and most of the patterns are real, but do not memorize them the way beginners do, as a catalog of magic incantations. The patterns matter because of what they reveal about who was in control during the bar. Internalize the four pieces of information in every candle, and you will independently rediscover most of the named patterns and understand them more deeply than the person who memorized them out of a book.

A few worth knowing by name, because they appear constantly. The doji, where open and close are essentially equal and the body is a thin line, says buyers and sellers fought to a draw. Its meaning depends entirely on context: a doji after a long uptrend can signal exhaustion of buying, a doji at the bottom of a downtrend can signal exhaustion of selling, a doji in the middle of a range means nothing. The pin bar, also called a hammer or shooting star, has a small body and a long wick, usually three or four times the body. A long wick below, at the bottom of a downtrend, is the hammer: sellers pushed down hard, but buyers reversed it within the bar. A long wick above, at the top of an uptrend, is the shooting star, the same story inverted. Pin bars are often early signals of trend exhaustion. The engulfing pattern is a two-bar formation, a small candle followed by a much larger one of the opposite color that completely engulfs the first body, and at the end of a trend it often marks a meaningful shift.

That is all you need on candle anatomy for now. Internalize the four pieces per bar, recognize the three or four named patterns at meaningful locations, and you have ninety percent of what candlestick analysis offers. The other ten percent is mostly people selling you indicators that translate the visual pattern into a number and then claim the number was the discovery. The nine on Marcus's chart, more or less.

From Bars to Structure: How a Trend Lives and Dies

A single candle is a moment. The chart is a sequence of moments. The structure that emerges from the sequence is where edge actually lives.

The simplest, most powerful concept in all of price action is also one of the easiest to state. An uptrend is a sequence of higher highs and higher lows. A downtrend is a sequence of lower highs and lower lows. Everything else is a range. Read that five times.

This framing is not new, and it is worth knowing where it comes from, because it tells you how durable it is. More than a century ago, Charles Dow, the man whose name is still on the Dow Jones average, built much of early technical theory on exactly this idea of trends defined by successive highs and lows. The vocabulary has multiplied since. The core has not changed, because it describes crowd behavior, and the crowd has not changed.

Why it matters: every trading strategy, no matter how sophisticated, is ultimately a bet on one of three things. The current trend continues, the current trend reverses, or the current range breaks out. If you cannot identify which of those three states the market is in, you cannot rationally choose between strategies. You will apply trend-following to a range and get whipsawed, or apply mean-reversion to a trend and get steamrolled.

The peak-and-trough method is how technicians categorize structure. Look at the chart over, say, the past twenty bars. Mark each significant swing high, a peak where the market reversed down, and each significant swing low, a trough where it reversed up. Then read the sequence. Higher highs and higher lows are an uptrend. Lower highs and lower lows is a downtrend. Swing highs and lows hitting roughly the same levels, oscillating without progress, is a range. Three states. You can describe any market on any timeframe in these terms.

What makes this useful is not only describing the current state but recognizing when it is changing. A trend does not end with a bell. It ends when the structure breaks. An uptrend has ended, structurally, when the market fails to make a new higher high and then breaks below the most recent higher low. The market has stopped going up, and the first piece of down-structure has fallen into place. It might not actually reverse; it might just consolidate and resume, but you cannot trade with the old trend any longer without admitting its structural integrity is gone. A downtrend has ended when the market fails to make a new lower low and then breaks above the most recent lower high—same logic, inverted. A range has broken out when price closes decisively outside its boundaries on increased volume, usually followed by a retest of the broken level as new support, if it broke up, or resistance, if it broke down.

Make this a daily habit. Look at the chart and ask: what is the structure right now? Is it intact? Is it weakening? Has it broken? If you cannot answer cleanly, you do not yet have an opinion on the market, and you should not be trading it.

Support and Resistance: The Memory of the Crowd

Here is something genuinely surprising about markets. They have memory. Specific price levels get visited and revisited, defended and attacked, broken and held, over spans that have no rational reason to matter. A price that was an important high in March quietly becomes an important price in September, even though nothing in the fundamentals connects the two moments.

The technical name for the levels where the market repeatedly stops and reverses is support and resistance, and these are some of the most useful pieces of information in technical analysis. They are also the easiest to identify, the easiest to abuse, and the most misunderstood. Support is a level where buying pressure has historically been strong enough to halt a decline, the floor of the room. Resistance is a level where selling pressure has historically been strong enough to halt an advance, the ceiling.

These levels exist for three overlapping reasons. First, market memory. Traders remember the prices at which they bought and sold. Someone who bought at $70 and watched it fall to $65 has unhappy memories of $70, and if the price climbs back, they often sell at breakeven to escape a position they regret. Multiply by thousands of traders with similar memories, and you get a self-organizing pool of supply around $70—second, psychological round numbers. Humans are not number-neutral. We treat $50 and $51 as basically the same, but $50 and $49 as crossing a line. Round numbers and round levels like 5,000 on the S&P attract attention, become reference points, and accumulate stops, targets, and orders until the clustering makes them act as support or resistance. Third, technical reference points. The previous day's high and low, the weekly high, the 200-day moving average, the level where a major pattern completes. Algorithms and discretionary traders alike watch these; orders cluster, and the clustering creates levels that look and behave like support and resistance.

The result is that certain levels acquire a kind of gravitational weight. The levels are not magic. The orders are real. The behavior is observable. The trick is reading the chart to find which levels matter and being honest enough to ignore the ones that do not.

A few principles for finding them well. More touches mean a stronger level; a level tested and held three or four times matters more than one tested once, and a level with five touches is essentially a wall. Recency matters; a level important six months ago and untouched since is much weaker than one tested yesterday, because memory fades and participants rotate. Higher timeframes win; a weekly level beats an hourly one, and if a daily resistance and a 15-minute support sit at the same price, trust the daily. Levels are zones, not lines. Beginners draw a single line at exactly $70.00 and feel betrayed when price reverses at $70.32, but a real level is a band, a few ticks in a tight market, a percent or two in a volatile one, so treat your levels as fat lines, not razor edges. And role reversal is real: when a strong support breaks, it almost always becomes resistance on the retest, and the reverse, because the traders who bought the old support are now underwater and sell to break even when price returns, creating supply at the level. This shows up so often it should be a default expectation, not a surprise.

Trend Lines and Channels

Static horizontal support and resistance are not the only memory in the market. There are also dynamic, angled lines that follow the trajectory of a trend, called trend lines. In an uptrend, you can usually draw a line connecting the successive higher lows, sloping up, and price tends to bounce off it on pullbacks because the trend's underlying demand is, on average, increasing at roughly the rate the line represents. As long as price respects the line, the uptrend is intact, and when price closes meaningfully below it the uptrend's integrity is compromised, not broken yet but weakened. In a downtrend, the equivalent line connects the successive lower highs, and a close above it is the first warning the downtrend may be ending.

Drawing trend lines is more art than science—a few rules. A trend line needs at least two touches to be a candidate and three to be confirmed, since two points define a line but the third proves it was not a coincidence. Use closing prices, not the absolute highs or lows of wicks, because wicks are noise and closes are decisions. Do not force the line; if the candidate requires you to ignore obvious violations, it is not a real trend line, so move on. And steeper lines break sooner than shallow ones; a near-vertical line is unsustainable and usually breaks within weeks, while a shallow one can run for months or years.

Draw a trend line and then a parallel line touching the corresponding highs, in an uptrend, or lows, in a downtrend, and you have a channel. Prices in strong trends often respect both edges, bouncing off the lower edge on pullbacks and reaching the upper edge on rallies, which makes channels useful for both entries: buy near the lower line in an uptrend, and take profits near the upper line. The reason it works is the same reason horizontal levels work. Enough participants watch the lines that orders cluster around them, and the clustering creates the very behavior the lines predict. This is the central truth of technical analysis. It works because it is widely believed. A self-fulfilling prophecy is still a real prophecy if you can be on the right side of it.

Volume: The Lie Detector

We touched volume in Chapter 3, on the plumbing. We return to it because volume is the single most important confirming signal in technical analysis, and most retail traders do not look at it carefully enough.

Recall the principle. A move on heavy volume is believed; a move on light volume is suspect. Now get specific. Trends should have volume aligned with their direction. In a healthy uptrend, the up-moves carry higher volume than the pullbacks, because the up-moves are the main event the participants are voting for with money and the pullbacks are the intermission, the profit-taking and hesitation. When the alignment breaks, the trend is weakening. If up-moves start happening on lower volume and pullbacks on higher volume, the market is telling you fewer people will bid it up, and more will sell into rallies so that the trend may run on momentum a while longer, but the fuel is going. This pattern, volume divergence, is one of the earliest reliable warnings of a reversal. Breakouts demand volume; a break of a range or a key level matters only on materially higher volume than the trading inside the range, and a thin breakout is much likelier to fail, the market saying "we crossed the line, but nobody meant it." And climaxes mark exhaustion: when a strong trend culminates in a massive volume spike, often three times or more the recent average, with price moving dramatically in the trend's direction, you are usually watching capitulation, the last holdouts forced in, the fuel all spent. Climaxes do not always mark the exact top or bottom but very often precede a major reversal within a short time, and recognizing them is one of the more lucrative pieces of pattern recognition you can develop.

A useful check every time you look at a chart: what is volume doing right now, and what does that tell me? Most retail traders study the price panel and ignore the volume bars underneath. Train yourself to see them. Volume often tells you the truth price action is hiding.

Multiple Timeframes: The Same Market Through Three Lenses

The single biggest leap in sophistication a developing trader makes is the moment they stop looking at a single chart and start looking at the same market on three timeframes at once. The technique is multiple timeframe analysis. Use a higher timeframe to determine the dominant trend: the weekly if you swing trade, the daily if you day trade. Use a middle timeframe to identify setups: the daily for swing trading, the 1-hour for day trading. Use a lower timeframe to time the actual entry: the 1-hour for swing trading, the 5- or 15-minute for day trading.

The discipline this enforces is enormous. The higher timeframe tells you which way the bias should run; I should only look for longs when the weekly is up, shorts when it is down. The middle timeframe tells you when a tradable setup is forming within that bias: the daily is pulling back to support; this could be a long. The lower timeframe tells you when the trigger has fired; the 1-hour just closed strongly off support on above-average volume, the trade is on. Without this hierarchy, traders constantly contradict themselves. They take a 5-minute long that conflicts with the 1-hour downtrend and get punished by the larger move. They buy a daily breakout that contradicts weekly resistance and watch it roll over. The lower timeframes are noisy and generate signals constantly, many of which are meaningless against the larger structure. The higher timeframes filter the noise and tell you which lower-timeframe signals deserve action.

A rule that has saved more traders than almost any other: the higher timeframe wins. When the 1-hour says buy, and the daily says downtrend, the daily wins. The 1-hour signal is one of many counter-trend setups that will fail individually until the daily trend itself changes. Trade with the higher timeframe or stand aside. Trading against it is statistically a losing proposition even when each signal looks compelling.

This rule is also, quietly, a survival tool inside an evaluation. Most of the impulsive trades that breach a daily loss limit are lower-timeframe signals taken against the higher-timeframe trend, the 5-minute bounce that felt urgent and ran straight into the daily downtrend. Dani's third evaluation died on exactly that, a cluster of counter-trend 5-minute longs that each looked compelling and collectively bled her past the line by lunch. The rule that would have saved her was not a better indicator. It was the willingness to let the higher timeframe overrule the urge. Which is less a charting skill than a nervous-system one, and which is the door to the other book.

The Limits of Technical Analysis

Let me close with a warning, because everything to this point has been about what technical analysis can do, and you deserve to know what it cannot.

Technical analysis assigns probabilities to short-term outcomes based on the recurring patterns of human behavior in markets. It works because human behavior in markets is, in fact, somewhat repetitive. Fear and greed leave similar footprints across decades and asset classes. The patterns are real. But there are situations where they do not apply, and the trader who refuses to recognize them gets eaten alive.

Surprise news breaks the pattern. When an unexpected geopolitical event, a surprise central-bank move, or a major data shock hits the wire, the technical landscape from five seconds ago is obsolete, and the levels that looked so solid get sliced like wet paper. Traders who defend their technical levels against a fundamental shock get carved up. The defense is awareness. Know what is on the economic calendar, know when the big announcements are scheduled, and either flatten or size down materially around them. Most "shocks" are actually scheduled events whose magnitude was underestimated. The truly unscheduled ones are rarer than people assume.

Low-volume markets distort everything. The patterns are reliable in liquid, active markets because they reflect many participants. In thin periods- overnight, holidays, sleepy summer afternoons- the patterns can lie, because they may reflect a handful of participants, and a "breakout" on a Friday afternoon in August on a thin contract may mean nothing more than one impatient algorithm lifting offers. Treat low-volume signals with extra skepticism, or do not trade them.

Structural shifts invalidate historical patterns. The patterns that formed on a human trading floor a generation ago are now shaped by algorithms working in milliseconds. The patterns persist because human psychology persists, but their shape and timing can change as the microstructure evolves. A working trader keeps recalibrating. And the patterns work because they are believed, so when too many traders crowd the same pattern in the same way, it stops working, or works too well at first and then disappoints. Markets adapt. Edges decay. Diversify your tools, update your understanding, and do not become religious about any single technique.

With those caveats firmly in mind, you have in this chapter the foundation of every technical tool you will ever use. Candles, structure, trend, support and resistance, trend lines and channels, volume confirmation, multiple timeframes. Combine them with discipline, and you can read essentially any chart in any market and form a reasoned hypothesis about its likely next move. Which is the moment, by the way, that the real difficulty begins, because reading the chart correctly and then doing the correct thing about it are two separate skills, run by two separate parts of you, and the gap between them is the whole subject of the other book.

In the next chapter we get more specific, moving from raw reading into the named, repeating patterns that recur across markets and across time, tell similar stories about the underlying psychology, and provide some of the highest-probability setups in the trader's playbook. They have names because they have been observed and traded for over a century. They are real. They are tradeable. They are also frequently abused. That is what we will fix.

CHAPTER 6, KEY IDEAS

- **Fundamentals and technicals are different lenses, not opposing religions.** Fundamentals tell you where prices should go eventually. Technicals tell you where they are going now. For leveraged short-term trading, the technical lens does most of the work, with fundamentals setting your broad orientation. Inside an evaluation, being right eventually does not count; the drawdown line resolves first.
- **Charts do not predict the future. They assign probabilities.** Anyone who tells you they know what the market will do is selling something.
- **Every candle holds four pieces of information:** direction, size, range, and close location within the range. Learn to read them and you re-derive most of the named patterns yourself, which beats stacking nine indicators on the chart.
- **Trend structure has three states:** uptrend, downtrend, and range. Every strategy is a bet on one of the three. Identifying the current state is the prerequisite for choosing a strategy. The framework goes back to Dow and survives because crowds do not change.
- **Support and resistance exist because markets have memory.** They are zones, not lines. More touches and more recent touches make them stronger. Broken support becomes resistance, and the reverse.
- **Trend lines and channels** track dynamic support and resistance, three touches to confirm. Steeper lines break sooner.
- **Volume is the lie detector.** Healthy trends carry higher volume on the trend moves than the pullbacks. Divergence is the earliest reliable warning. Breakouts demand volume. Climaxes mark exhaustion.
- **Multiple timeframe analysis is the leap to seriousness, and a survival tool.** Higher timeframe sets bias, middle finds setups, lower times entries. The higher timeframe wins, and most evaluation-killing impulse trades are lower-timeframe signals taken against it. It cost Dani an account to learn it.
- **Technical analysis has limits.** Surprise news breaks patterns, thin markets distort them, microstructure evolves, and

crowded patterns lose their edge. Stay humble, stay current, never trade a chart religiously.

CHAPTER 7

The Shapes of Crowds

Once Marcus learned to read price, he developed the opposite problem. He could see patterns everywhere.

He sent Sal a chart with five formations drawn on it, the same forty bars carved into a head and shoulders, a double bottom, a triangle, a flag, and a wedge, depending on which points he chose to connect. He was, he thought, finally seeing the market. "I see all of it now," he wrote. Sal, who had watched a hundred young traders pass through this exact fever, wrote back: "You see a cloud, and you found a rabbit, a face, and a sailboat in it. The market generates a pattern every few minutes. Your job is not to find them. Your job is to ignore almost all of them."

That is the real subject of this chapter. Not the patterns. The discipline of which ones to trade, and the larger number to walk past. Hold that line, because it is also, as Dani is about to discover, the exact discipline an evaluation is built to break.

Markets are made of people, and people, it turns out, do roughly the same things in roughly the same situations across decades and centuries. This is the only reason chart patterns work. The price of a futures contract is set by the collective behavior of thousands of participants deciding in real time. When they face a particular situation- the market has rallied for weeks, every recent push higher has hit a wall of sellers at this level, now we are approaching that level again- they tend to behave in similar ways. Some hold, some take profits, some flip short. The resulting price action looks, on the chart, similar to the last time the same situation arose. Not identical. But similar enough that, with enough exposure, you can recognize the situation and form a probabilistic guess about what comes next.

That is the entire intellectual basis of pattern trading. It is not magic, and it is not numerology. It is recognition that human group psychology, in the specific environment of a financial market, produces recurrent statistical regularities. Recognize them, trade them with discipline, do not become religious about any single one.

Chart patterns sort cleanly into two families that tell two different stories. Reversal patterns appear at the end of trends, the visual signature of a market that has been running one direction and is now running out of fuel. They mark the transition from one trend to the opposite, or at least into a meaningful pause. Continuation patterns appear in the middle of trends, the signature of a market taking a brief breath before resuming, and they offer some of the lowest-risk entries in the trader's playbook.

The goal here is not to memorize fifty patterns. It is to understand the deep logic of how patterns form, so you can recognize them in the non-textbook shapes they almost always actually appear in.

Reversal Patterns: The Shape of Trends Ending

A reversal pattern marks where the dominant trend's underlying demand, or supply, starts to fail. Volume slows. The leading direction gets harder to defend. A new tribe, the ones who believe the trend has gone too far, starts entering on the opposite side. The pattern is the chart's record of the battle, and its resolution is the moment one tribe wins.

A few principles apply to every reversal pattern. They take time; a reversal is not a single bar but typically weeks or months on the daily, or hours on the intraday, and patterns that try to form too fast almost always fail. Volume confirms, declining as the pattern develops, showing waning conviction in the old trend, and surging on the breakout, showing fresh conviction in the new direction. Higher timeframes are more reliable; a weekly reversal means far more than a 15-minute one. And the breakout, not the formation, is what you trade; the pattern by itself is just a suspicion, the resolution is the signal, so wait for it.

The head and shoulders is the most famous reversal pattern in technical analysis, and it earned its fame the hard way, by working with surprising reliability for over a century. It marks the top of an uptrend with three peaks. The middle peak, the head, is the highest. The two flanking peaks, the shoulders, are roughly equal and both lower than the head. Connecting the two lows between the peaks gives the neckline, the level that triggers the pattern when broken. In slow motion: the market rallies to a high, retraces, rallies to a higher high, retraces; that is the left shoulder and the first leg of the head. It rallies again to the new high of the head and pulls back to roughly the same low, establishing the neckline. Nothing alarming yet. Then the next rally fails, reaching only a level below the head, the right shoulder, the first structural sign the trend is broken, a failure to make a higher high. The market sells off toward the neckline again, and the pattern completes when price breaks decisively below it. The trade is clean: short on the neckline break, ideally with a volume surge; stop above the right shoulder, or more conservatively above the head; target the vertical distance from head to neckline, projected downward from the break. The inverse head and shoulders is the same pattern flipped: three troughs, marking the bottom of a downtrend, same mechanics inverted. The psychology is why it works. The head is the last successful push by the trend's buyers, the strongest hands making one more attempt with the last of their ammunition. The right shoulder is the failure, the same buyers unable even to match the previous high. Profit-takers sell, the neckline breaks, the deeper sellers who waited for confirmation pile in, and the reversal is set in motion. Every step has a clear behavioral logic. That is why it persists.

Double tops and double bottoms are simpler and even more common. A double top has two peaks at roughly the same level with a valley between; the second peak is the trend's failed attempt to push to a new high, stalling at the first peak's level. The valley defines the support line, and the pattern completes when price breaks below it. The story is that buyers tried twice and failed both times; the level became a wall, and sellers gained confidence. Entry on the support break, stop above the second peak, target the distance from peaks to the intermediate low projected down from the break. Double bottoms work the same in reverse. A triple top or bottom is the same idea with three tests, rarer than doubles but more reliable when they appear, because three failed tests is a stronger statement than two. Note what "roughly the same level" means in practice. The two peaks do not need to match exactly; a real double top often has peaks differing by a percent or two, the structural point being that both failed to extend the trend. If the second peak is dramatically lower, you may be looking at a forming right shoulder, not a double top. If it is dramatically higher, the trend has not failed; it merely paused.

The rounding top and rounding bottom, the latter sometimes called a saucer, are less dramatic but equally meaningful. No sharp peaks, just slow, gradual curves, the price losing momentum over weeks or months, drifting sideways or slightly higher, then drifting back down, all without a dramatic single event, an inverted bowl on the chart. The trend does not break; it fades. These are easier to recognize in retrospect than in real time, which limits their tradeability. Still, they are worth understanding because they represent a particular kind of trend death, gradual and almost peaceful. You will rarely trade them directly, but recognizing one gives you situational awareness. A market two months into a rounding top is not one you want to be aggressively long, even if no single dramatic signal has fired.

Continuation Patterns: The Shape of Trends Resting

Now the other family. A continuation pattern appears when a market in a strong trend pauses, consolidates briefly, then resumes. The mechanic is always the same. The market has been moving aggressively. Trend buyers or sellers pause to digest, profit-takers exit, short-term contrarians try to fade the move, and volume declines as participation moderates. Price moves sideways or in a small countertrend for a brief period, usually shorter than a comparable reversal. Then the original trend reasserts, often with a sharp breakout on volume. These are valuable because they offer low-risk entries into established trends. You missed the original move; the continuation pattern gives you a second chance at better risk-reward than chasing the original breakout would have.

A few principles for all of them. They are shorter than reversal patterns; a flag might take three to ten bars while a head and shoulders takes months, consistent with the story, a pause rather than a structural change. Volume should decline during the pattern and surge on the breakout. The breakout direction matches the prior trend; trading these against the prior trend is a losing proposition. And the expected move after the pattern is at least as large as the move that preceded it, the measured-move principle that makes them tradeable with defined targets.

Flags are the most common continuation pattern on any market and timeframe. A sharp directional move, the flagpole, then a brief consolidation drifting in a tight channel slightly against the trend, the flag, then the trend resumes with a breakout in the original direction, often moving a distance about equal to the flagpole. A bullish flag has an upward pole and a slightly down or sideways flag, breaking up. A bearish flag is the inverse. Wait for the breakout; do not anticipate it, since many flag-like consolidations resolve as reversals. Enter on the breakout, or on the first pullback to the broken boundary. Stop at the opposite end of the flag. Target the flagpole length projected from the breakout. The clean flag's risk-reward is often 1 to 3 or better, which is why these are the bread and butter of disciplined trend traders.

Pennants are structurally similar, but the consolidation is triangular rather than rectangular, the price coiling tighter as it develops. The apex is the moment of decision, and the breakout is usually sharp, the coiling compressing energy that releases violently. Entry on the breakout in the prior trend's direction, stop at the opposite side, target the prior leg projected from the breakout. In practice, flags and pennants are often grouped, and the distinction matters less than you might think.

Triangles are more general consolidations over a longer period than a flag or pennant, in three flavors. An ascending triangle has a flat upper boundary and a rising lower boundary, usually resolving up as rising lows show buying pressure overwhelming static resistance. A descending triangle is the mirror, flat support and falling highs, usually resolving down. A symmetrical triangle has both boundaries converging, lower highs and higher lows, with no inherent bias, so wait for the breakout direction to reveal itself. Same rules across all three: wait for the breakout, enter in its direction, stop at the opposite boundary, target the triangle's widest height projected from the breakout. One nuance: as a triangle nears its apex, it loses predictive power, and it is most reliable when the breakout comes in the middle two-thirds of its depth.

Rectangles, what most traders call a range, oscillate between clearly defined horizontal support and resistance for an extended period.

They can form as continuation patterns within a trend, resolving in the trend's direction, or as standalone environments, a market simply not trending, where the range itself is the structure. In a trend, expect resolution in the prior direction with a measured move equal to the rectangle's height. In a non-trend, the range defines a different approach: buying near support, selling near resistance, stops just outside the boundaries, until the breakout invalidates the range. The discipline is not to predict the breakout direction. Wait. The trader who tries to anticipate it usually loses, because the whole point of a range is that nobody knows.

Wedges look like a triangle whose boundaries both slope the same way. A rising wedge has both boundaries sloping up, the upper rising more slowly than the lower. It looks bullish, with higher highs and higher lows. Still, it is usually bearish, because the slowing pace of higher highs against the steeper rise of higher lows shows the upward thrust exhausting itself, and it typically resolves with a downward break, often sharp, even in an uptrend. A falling wedge is the inverse; it looks bearish, usually breaks up. The counter-intuitive direction is what catches traders off-guard. Trade the wedge on its resolution, not its appearance.

Pattern Reliability: The Honest Math

So far I have presented the patterns the way most textbooks do, as if they always work. Here are the honest numbers, because this is one area where salesman-style trading books mislead beginners spectacularly. In rigorous historical studies, the success rates are not the 80 or 90% sometimes claimed. The best-case high-quality patterns, clean structure, strong volume confirmation, formed at major support or resistance, aligned with the higher-timeframe trend, succeed in the 60 to 70% range. Average patterns, recognizable but with mixed confirmation in less ideal locations, around 50%. Marginal patterns, forced, weak volume, at no particular level, against the higher-timeframe trend, 30 to 40% or worse. (*These are honest ranges from the pattern literature, not precise constants.*)

Even the best patterns fail one time in three. Internalize that. Pattern trading is not about being right. It is about being correct more often than the math requires while controlling losses on the failures. A 60% win rate on a 1-to-2 setup is enormously profitable over time.

But the 40% of the time the pattern fails, you must take the loss with the same discipline you used to take the entry. The trader who refuses to honor stops on failed patterns blows up the strategy even when the pattern itself was sound. Notice that the failure point is never the chart. It is the person reading it. We will spend the back of this book, and the whole of the next one, on that person.

This is why the context around a pattern matters more than the pattern. The same head and shoulders in two different contexts has wildly different probabilities. Grade every pattern against six questions. Is it at a meaningful level? A pattern completing at major support or resistance is much stronger than one in the middle of nowhere. Is it confirmed on multiple timeframes? The same pattern visible on the hourly and daily is far stronger than one only on the 15-minute. Does the volume align, declining during formation and surging on the breakout? Does it align with the higher-timeframe trend? A continuation pattern with the dominant trend is high probability; a reversal against a strong dominant trend is low probability. Did it take time to form? A head and shoulders over eight weeks beats one over four days. And are there conflicting signals: a major release, a pending Fed decision, a geopolitical event in progress, any of which can invalidate a pattern. A setup that ticks all six is a high-conviction trade you can size appropriately. One that ticks two or three is a marginal trade you should probably skip. Grading every pattern against this checklist before placing the trade is the difference between a strategy that wins and one that quietly bleeds.

Pattern Failures: The Trades That Define You

Every pattern fails sometimes, and how you handle the failure determines whether you survive. A pattern fails when it does the opposite of what it suggested: a head and shoulders that breaks the neckline down, then immediately reverses back above the right shoulder; a bullish flag that breaks up, then collapses through its support; a double bottom that breaks up, then rolls back over. Failures happen regularly, in every pattern type, regardless of how clean the setup looked. This is not a flaw; it is a feature of probabilistic trading. The question is what you do about it.

Three rules. Honor your stops: the same religion from Chapter 4. The stop you set was the level at which the setup is invalidated, so if price reaches it, the pattern has failed, and you exit; you do not give it more time, you do not move the stop, you exit, take the loss, and hunt the next setup. Recognize the failure quickly, since failed patterns often produce sharp, fast moves the opposite way. If you spot the failure within a few bars, a breakout that immediately reverses on heavy volume, you exit at a much smaller loss than waiting for the formal stop. And failed patterns often become contrary signals: when a clean pattern breaks the wrong way decisively, the participants who positioned for it have to unwind, providing fuel for an explosive move in the opposite direction, which should not be your primary strategy but should not be ignored either.

One Last Warning: The Patterns You See vs. the Patterns That Are There

Humans are pattern-recognition machines. Mostly an advantage. In trading, a profound liability, because the same machinery that lets us see real patterns fabricates patterns where none exist. Stare at a chart long enough, and you can find a head and shoulders, a double bottom, a triangle, a wedge, and a flag in the same chart, depending on which points you emphasize. This is overfitting, the most common pathology of self-taught technicians, and it is exactly the chart Marcus sent Sal. They see signals everywhere, take trades constantly, overtrade, lose more than they win, and conclude the patterns do not work, when in fact the patterns are real, and they were not selective enough.

The discipline is selectivity. The market generates patterns continuously, and most of them are noise. Your job is not to trade every pattern you can see. It is to trade the small number that pass the quality checklist with high marks. "No, I will not trade this. Yes, I will trade that" is the most important judgment a pattern trader makes, and the trades you do not take matter as much as the ones you do. A useful rule of thumb: if you are trading more than two or three patterns a week across all your contracts and timeframes, you are probably overtrading. Real high-conviction setups are not that common. If you are seeing them constantly, you are manufacturing them. Slow down. Be picky. Wait for the clear ones.

The Target Trap: How an Evaluation Manufactures Patterns

Now watch what happens to that discipline when somebody attaches a number to it.

Dani knew all of this. She could grade a setup against the six questions in her sleep, and on her own small account she traded as Sal taught her to, two or three clean ones a week, long stretches of nothing in between. Then she bought her fifth evaluation, and the firm gave her a profit target and a clock. Hit a fixed dollar amount to pass. The clock was not formal, but it was real, because every day she sat flat was a day the fee she had paid earned nothing and the target sat there unmet, and the part of her that wanted to be funded started reading the gap between her account and the target as a debt that was coming due.

So she went looking. Not for the clean setups, those had not changed their frequency just because she needed them to. She went looking for setups, period, and a mind that goes looking for patterns finds them, because that is what the machinery does. A sideways drift she would have ignored on Tuesday became, on a Thursday with the target unmet, an ascending triangle. A weak two-bar pause became a flag. She was not lying to herself, not exactly. She was lowering the grade she would accept, one tick at a time, because the alternative was sitting still while the number she needed refused to come to her. By Friday she had taken nine trades in a market that had offered maybe one, and the small losses on the eight marginal ones had walked her straight into the trailing drawdown. The evaluation did not end on a bad chart. It ended on a manufactured one.

This is the target trap, and it is one of the most reliable ways a capable trader fails an evaluation, because it does not feel like recklessness. It feels like effort. It feels like trying harder, doing more, chasing the goal the way you were taught to chase goals everywhere else in your life. Every other arena rewards more activity in pursuit of a number. This one punishes it. The target makes you trade, and trading more in a market that is not offering setups is precisely how you hand your edge back.

The move is the one Sal had been teaching her all along, only now it had to survive the pressure of the target. Process is the goal, not the number. A no-trade day is a valid plan, not a failure of nerve. You judge the session by the rules you kept, not the dollars you booked, because over a large enough sample the kept rules produce the dollars and the chased dollars produce the drawdown. When Dani finally passed, on her sixth evaluation, she passed by trading less. She set a hard cap on trades per day; she wrote "the target is none of my business, my rules are my only business" at the top of her journal, and she let the clock run out on three separate days without taking a thing. The target came to her in the end, the way it comes to everyone who stops chasing it, slowly and then suddenly.

If you are trading an evaluation, this tendency has a name: patience under a target, and it is the single behavior most likely to end an attempt. Dani's whole arc comes due at the Funded Account chapter. For now, hold the principle: the number is bait, the rules are the edge, and selectivity does not get less important when the stakes go up. It gets more important, and exactly that much harder to hold, which is the part *Trade Calm* exists to train.

Patient Traders and Anxious Chart-Readers

This is what separates patient pattern traders from anxious chart-readers. The patient ones wait—the anxious ones force. The patient ones make money over years. The anxious ones provide the liquidity the patient ones make money on. Marcus, at this point in his story, was firmly in the second group, and the thing standing between him and the first was not another pattern. It was the wiring that made waiting feel unbearable, which is precisely the wiring Trade Calm is built to retrain. Dani was a year ahead of him on the same road, and even she had to be broken by a target before the lesson finally set. The selectivity is simple to understand and brutal to execute, and the execution is not a charting skill. It is a nervous-system one.

In the next chapter we move from the visual world of patterns into the numerical world of indicators, the moving averages, oscillators, momentum measures, and volume tools that distill price into computed signals. Indicators are useful when used carefully. They are also one of the most heavily marketed and heavily abused categories in the entire industry. It is where Marcus put his nine pairs of sunglasses. We will sort the real from the noise.

CHAPTER 7, KEY IDEAS

- **Chart patterns work because human psychology is repetitive.** Markets are made of people; people do similar things in similar situations, and the chart records the result.
- **Reversal patterns** mark the end of trends: head and shoulders and its inverse, double and triple tops and bottoms, and the slower rounding tops and bottoms.
- **Continuation patterns** mark pauses in trends: flags, pennants, triangles (ascending, descending, symmetrical), rectangles, and wedges. Counter-intuitively, rising wedges break down and falling wedges break up.
- **The breakout, not the formation, is what you trade.** The pattern alone is a suspicion. Its resolution is the signal.
- **Volume confirms patterns.** Declining during formation, surging on breakout. Without it, treat the pattern as suspect.
- **Realistic reliability:** best-quality patterns succeed about 60 to 70% of the time, average ones about 50%, marginal ones 30 to 40%. Every pattern fails sometimes. Honor your stops without exception, because the failure point is always the person, never the chart.
- **Pattern quality is everything.** Grade each setup against six criteria: meaningful level, multiple-timeframe confirmation, volume alignment, higher-timeframe trend alignment, time to form, and a clear calendar.
- **Failed patterns are themselves tradeable.** A clean pattern that breaks the wrong way often produces explosive moves the other direction as the original positioners unwind.
- **Selectivity is the discipline.** Most patterns you see are noise. Two or three real high-conviction setups a week is plenty. If you are seeing them constantly, you are manufacturing them.
- **The target trap is selectivity's enemy inside an evaluation.** A profit target makes you go looking for setups, and a mind that goes looking finds them, lowering its standards one tick at a time until marginal trades bleed it into the drawdown. The move: process is the goal, a no-trade day is a valid plan, and you judge the session by the rules you kept. It took Dani an evaluation to pass by trading less.

CHAPTER 8

The Indicator Trap

It is time to deal with Marcus's nine indicators.

Open any modern trading platform and within about ninety seconds you are confronted by a menu of technical indicators that runs into the dozens. The household names, moving averages, RSI, MACD, Bollinger Bands, stochastics, and then the exotic specimens that someone, somewhere, was paid to invent: the Vortex Indicator, the Aroon Oscillator, the Klinger Volume Oscillator, the Mass Index, the Coppock Curve. There are platforms with over a hundred built in. There are subscription services that will sell you "proprietary" indicators built on top of the public ones for $99 a month. There is a vibrant cottage industry of online traders demonstrating, with breathtaking confidence, that the secret to consistent profits is the correct combination of three or four of these with the correct parameter settings. This is the swamp Marcus wandered into, and the one Sal told him to climb out of.

Almost none of it matters. Most of it is noise. Some of it is malpractice. A small, important subset is genuinely useful, and the difference between the useful and the rest is the entire subject of this chapter.

Here is the first thing to understand, and take it personally before we go a step further. Indicators are not signals from the market. Indicators are mathematical transformations of price data. Everything an indicator "tells" you was already present in the price action. The indicator re-expresses it in a different visual form. A moving average is a smoothed version of the price. The RSI is the price's rate of change normalized to a 0 to 100 scale. The MACD is the difference between two moving averages, dressed up with a third. None of these contain information the price chart does not already contain. They contain rearrangements of it.

This matters because indicators are often marketed, implicitly or explicitly, as if they generate new information about the market. They do not. They show you what was already there, in a form that makes some patterns easier to see and some easier to miss. A good indicator highlights something useful that was hard to see directly. A bad indicator drowns the useful pattern in noise. Most indicators are bad, most traders use too many, and most charts I see from intermediate traders are an unreadable mess of overlapping lines and oscillators, none of which the trader could justify if pressed. Marcus could not justify a single one of his nine.

The discipline is to choose a small number of indicators, three or four maximum, that each serve a clear purpose, to understand exactly what each tells you and what it does not, and to use that small set consistently across many trades. The trader who switches indicators every week hunting for the magic combination is doing astrology. The trader who uses two or three for years, refining his understanding of how each behaves in different conditions, is doing engineering. Let me show you the small set that matters, and tell you what each is good for and what each is good for nothing.

The Moving Average: The Most Useful Indicator Ever Invented

A moving average is the simplest possible indicator. It is the average of the closing prices over the last N bars, plotted as a continuous line that updates with each new bar. That is it. Nothing mysterious. The simplicity is its strength. It smooths the random oscillations of price into a single line that represents the trend over the chosen period. The longer the period, the smoother the line and the more it represents long-term direction. The shorter, the more responsive and the more it tracks short-term swings. The 20-period gives the short-term trend, the 50-period the medium, the 200-period the long. Almost every meaningful piece of moving-average analysis comes down to those three.

There are variations: the exponential weights recent prices more heavily and respond faster, the weighted uses a linear scheme, the adaptive flavors adjust smoothing to volatility. For our purposes, the differences matter less than you would think. The simple moving average is fine for most applications and is the version I will reference. Once you understand what a moving average is doing, you can substitute any flavor you prefer.

What can it tell you? Direction: sloping up, the price is in an uptrend over the lookback; down, a downtrend; flat, a range. This sounds trivial, but the discipline of saying "the 50-day is rising, therefore I am only looking for long setups on this contract" eliminates an enormous category of bad trades. Dynamic support and resistance: in a trend, price tends to pull back to the moving average before resuming; the 20-period is often the first stop on a pullback, the 50 the second, the 200 the line whose break marks a major regime change, and it works for the same reason horizontal levels work: enough traders watch it that orders cluster. Trend strength: the slope is a rough measure of force; a steeply rising 50-day is a stronger trend than a gently rising one, and when the slope flattens, the trend is weakening. Trend alignment: when the short, medium, and long are stacked in the right order, 20 above 50 above 200 for an uptrend and the reverse for a downtrend, the trend has confirmation across all three, and when they cross or tangle the market is in transition or range.

The most famous moving-average signal is the crossover. The Golden Cross, the 50-day crossing above the 200, is read as bullish. The Death Cross, the 50 below the 200, is bearish. Both have a respectable record on major indices and a less respectable one on individual contracts. Let me be honest about crossovers. They are late. By definition, a crossover happens after the trend has already changed, the moving averages lag, and the cross confirms a change that has already begun rather than predicting one about to occur. Wait for the Golden Cross to go long the S&P, and you have missed the first chunk of the rally. The signal is real, but the entry is poor. Crossovers are most useful as confirming signals for a thesis you already had, or as trend filters telling you the broad bias.

The single most valuable use of the moving average is the simplest, as a bias filter. If the 50-day is rising, I only take long setups. If falling, only shorts. If flat, I stand aside or trade range strategies. This one rule, applied with discipline, would save more retail traders than almost any other piece of advice in this book. Most losing trades happen because the trader was fighting the dominant trend, and the moving average is the dominant trend, made visible.

The RSI: The Most Misunderstood Indicator Ever Invented

The Relative Strength Index, the RSI, was published in 1978 by J. Welles Wilder Jr., a mechanical engineer turned trader who in the same book introduced several indicators we still use. It is a momentum oscillator that compares the magnitude of recent gains to recent losses, normalized to a 0 to 100 scale, with a standard lookback of 14 bars. Traditionally, above 70 is "overbought" and may be due for a pullback; below 30 is "oversold" and may be due for a bounce. That is the version most beginners learn and then proceed to use catastrophically badly.

Here is the trap. The naive interpretation, the RSI is above 70 therefore the market is going down, is, in a trending market, an excellent way to lose money. A strong uptrend can keep the RSI pinned above 70 for weeks. Every "overbought" reading you take as a short will be punished by the trend continuing up. The same applies to downtrends and oversold readings. RSI extremes do not mean trade against the trend. They often mean the trend is so strong the indicator cannot contain it. Trading the RSI naively against strong trends is one of the most destructive things a developing trader can do.

The correct interpretation is not overbought or oversold. It is a measurement of momentum, and momentum behaves differently in different contexts. In a ranging market, the RSI is genuinely useful for timing entries within the range: buying near the bottom when RSI is below 30, selling near the top when above 70; the range defines the structure, and the RSI fine-tunes the entry, which is the original use Wilder envisioned. In a trending market, the RSI is most useful not at the extremes but in the middle of its range, the 40 to 60 band, the trend zone. In a healthy uptrend, RSI pullbacks tend to bottom around 40, and when the RSI breaks below 40 in a supposed uptrend, the momentum has materially weakened. In a healthy downtrend, RSI rallies tend to top around 60. The 40 and 60 boundaries are far more informative than the 30 and 70 extremes.

Divergence is the RSI's most genuinely valuable signal. Divergence is when the indicator moves opposite to price. Price makes a new high, but the RSI makes a lower high, bearish divergence: the price still extending up but the underlying momentum weakening, one of the most reliable early warnings of an impending reversal at the end of a strong uptrend. The inverse, bullish divergence, price making new lows while RSI makes higher lows, is its mirror at the end of downtrends. But divergence is not by itself a signal to trade against the trend. It is a warning to start watching price more carefully. Confirmation still has to come from price: a break of structure, a meaningful close against the trend, a pattern resolution. Divergence is the early warning, price action is the trigger. Trade them in that order, and you have a powerful technique. Trade divergence alone and you will frequently be early, which in trading is the same as wrong.

A few more RSI techniques worth knowing. You can draw trend lines on the RSI itself, and when it breaks its own trend line, the momentum supporting the price trend has shifted, often before the price's trend line breaks. There are failure swings, when the RSI rises above 70, pulls back, fails to make a new high above 70, then breaks the intermediate low, a momentum confirmation of a reversal, inverse for bullish. And the 50 line itself is meaningful; in an uptrend the RSI should stay predominantly above 50, and when it breaks decisively below and stays there the momentum has flipped, a coarser but more reliable signal than the extremes. The honest summary: the RSI is a momentum indicator, not a reversal indicator. Use it to confirm trend strength, to spot divergence, and to time entries within ranges. Do not use it as a standalone signal to trade against the dominant trend. That path leads to ruin.

The MACD: The Workhorse

The Moving Average Convergence Divergence, the MACD, was created by Gerald Appel in the late 1970s. It is the most widely used momentum indicator in professional trading, and unlike many, it has earned its popularity. It has three components: the MACD line, the difference between the 12-period and 26-period EMAs of price; the signal line, the 9-period EMA of the MACD line; and the histogram, the difference between the MACD line and the signal line, plotted as bars above and below zero. That is the standard parameter set: 12, 26, 9, and roughly a billion words have been written debating whether other parameters are better. Spare yourself the journey. The standard parameters work fine. Customizing them is the digital equivalent of polishing the chrome on a car that never leaves the driveway.

What it tells you. The MACD line above zero means the 12-EMA is above the 26-EMA; the short-term trend is bullish relative to the medium; below zero, the opposite; the zero line is a momentum divider. The MACD line crossing above the signal line is a bullish momentum signal, crossing below bearish, and these crossovers are the most commonly traded MACD events, lagging like all moving-average signals but clean, mechanical, and easy to backtest. The histogram is the most useful and most underused element, the bars getting taller as the MACD line accelerates away from the signal line and shorter as it decelerates and approaches, giving you a real-time read on the rate of change of momentum, whether the trend is accelerating or losing steam. Shrinking histogram bars are the earliest warning a crossover is coming, often several bars ahead. Watching the histogram is, in my view, the single most valuable thing you can do with the MACD. And MACD divergence works the same as RSI divergence and is just as useful, particularly reliable on the daily chart at major turning points.

The MACD's main weakness, like all moving-average tools, is choppy sideways markets, where it generates a stream of false crossovers as the short and medium EMAs whip past each other. It works best in trends. In ranges, set it aside or use only its divergence. The most useful combination I have ever seen is the MACD plus a 200-period moving average. The 200 tells you the dominant long-term trend, the MACD the short-to-medium momentum. Trade only MACD signals that align with the 200's direction. Bullish crossover above the 200, take it. Bullish crossover below the 200, ignore it; it is counter-trend. This single rule, only trade MACD signals in the direction of the 200, is the spine of more profitable systems than almost any other combination I know. Simple, mechanical, it works.

The Stochastic, Bollinger Bands, and the Volume Tools

A few more, more briefly, because much of what was said above transfers directly.

The Stochastic Oscillator, developed by George Lane in the 1950s, is a finer-grained alternative to the RSI. Both fluctuate between 0 and 100, both flag overbought and oversold, both produce divergences. The Stochastic compares the current close to the price range over a lookback: a close near the high of the range reading near 100, near the low near 0, plotted as the %K line, with a 3-period average called %D alongside for smoothing. Where the RSI smooths gradually, the Stochastic is more reactive, picking up turns earlier but producing more false signals, so the RSI is better for slower longer-timeframe work and the Stochastic for faster shorter-timeframe entries. The most useful technique is %K crossing %D inside the extreme zones, both lines below 20 and %K crossing up through %D as a buy, more reliable than a simple below-20 reading because the crossover confirms momentum actually turned. Use it for divergence, respect the dominant trend, treat the extremes as alerts, not signals. It is a good tool, not magic. And do not run it alongside the RSI. Pick one.

John Bollinger introduced his bands in the early 1980s. A band is built around a moving average, typically 20-period, with upper and lower bands at a fixed number of standard deviations, typically two, so the envelope expands when volatility increases and contracts when it decreases. The width measures volatility, and the contraction, the Bollinger squeeze, is the most useful signal, dramatic narrowing indicating unusually low volatility that historically tends to precede explosive moves in either direction, the squeeze telling you to watch for the breakout without telling you the direction. Price touching the upper band means it has moved about two standard deviations from its average. The naive read is a sell signal, but like the RSI it depends on context, and in a strong trend price can and frequently does ride a band for extended periods, so selling against a price hugging the upper band in a strong uptrend is the same mistake as shorting an overbought RSI. Price closing back inside the bands after a breach is a more reliable mean-reversion signal than the touch itself. The middle band acts as dynamic support and resistance like any moving average. Bollinger Bands are particularly useful for range traders and less useful for trend traders, who should care more about the moving average and momentum.

There is also a family of volume indicators. On-Balance Volume, from Joe Granville in the 1960s, is a running total, adding the period's volume on an up close and subtracting on a down close; the value is in divergence when price makes new highs, but OBV does not; the volume is not supporting the move. Volume-Weighted Average Price, VWAP, is the average price weighted by volume over a period, usually the day, the price at which the average dollar of volume changed hands, used by institutions as a benchmark and by retail traders mostly as an intraday support and resistance level, with a pullback to VWAP in an intraday trend often a good entry. The Money Flow Index is essentially the RSI with volume incorporated, and if you already use the RSI, it is redundant, so use one or the other, not both. A general note: volume indicators are most useful in equity markets and major liquid contracts, and in thin overnight futures sessions they can produce unreliable signals, so always check whether the contract has meaningful volume in the period you are analyzing.

The Average True Range: The Indicator You Will Use Every Day

The Average True Range, the ATR, is another Wilder invention from 1978, and it might be the single most useful indicator in this entire chapter, precisely because it does not try to generate trade signals at all. It measures one thing. Volatility. The True Range for a single bar is the largest of three numbers: the current bar's high minus low, the absolute value of the current high minus the previous close, and the absolute value of the current low minus the previous close, so it captures both the bar's range and any gap from the prior close. The ATR is a moving average, typically over 14 periods, of the True Range, a single number representing the typical bar's range over the recent past. On a daily crude chart, an ATR of $1.50 means daily ranges have averaged about $1.50 a barrel.

Why it matters: the ATR is the trader's universal yardstick for setting stops, position sizes, and profit targets that scale with the market's actual volatility. A common rule for stop placement is that the stop equals two times ATR below the entry for a long, the ATR stop, reasoning that if the typical bar range is X then a stop within X will be hit by ordinary noise, while a stop at 2X is far enough to survive random fluctuation but close enough to cut losses promptly, with aggressive traders using 1.5X and conservative ones 3X. The same logic applies to targets and trailing stops: an initial target of entry plus three times ATR is a defensible default for a 1.5 to 1 setup, and a trailing stop of current price minus two times ATR maintains a constant, volatility-adjusted distance. The deeper value is that the ATR lets you size positions consistently across markets with wildly different price scales and volatilities. A 2-ATR stop on a quiet currency contract might be 30 pips, on a volatile crude contract $3.00, both the same relative risk to the market's normal behavior. Sizing so that dollar risk, position size times stop distance, is constant across trades, which is the whole point of position sizing from Chapter 4, requires knowing the volatility of each contract, and the ATR gives you that number directly. If I had to pick a single indicator and discard the rest, it would be the ATR. Not because it predicts anything-it does not, but because it makes everything else you do quantitatively meaningful.

There is a quiet bonus for the funded trader here. The ATR is also the cleanest way to know, before you place a single order, whether a contract even fits the account you are trading. If the typical daily range in dollars is large relative to the loss limit you are working under, the market can stop you out on an ordinary day through no fault of your own, and the honest move is a smaller contract or a different market. Dani sizes every evaluation this way now. She checks the ATR against the trailing drawdown first, and if the math says one normal day of noise can breach the line, she trades the micro, or she trades something quieter. It is not a glamorous use of an indicator. It is the unglamorous that keeps an account.

The Honest Stack: Three Indicators, Used Well

I have discussed at least seven indicators in this chapter. Let me collapse all of it into the small, honest stack I would actually recommend. Three. A 200-period moving average for trend, telling you the dominant direction; take only trades aligned with it. The MACD for momentum, the histogram for early shifts, the crossover for confirmation, divergences for reversal warnings. And the ATR for volatility, telling you how to size positions, set stops, and place targets properly scaled to the market.

That is it. With this stack, you can determine the dominant trend, filter out counter-trend setups, time entries on momentum shifts, spot weakening trends and possible reversals, and size positions and set stops that respect each market's actual behavior. This is the indicator framework of a working professional. It is not flashy. It will not sell any newsletter subscriptions. It is, however, more or less what people who make money for a living actually use. The traders with twenty indicators on the screen are, in my experience, not the ones making money. They are usually some version of Marcus three weeks in, wearing nine pairs of sunglasses indoors.

Dani's chart used to look like Marcus's. Early on she ran a dozen indicators, and like everyone who does, she found that for any decision she wanted to make, at least one of the twelve agreed with her, which is not analysis; it is permission. Part of what steadied her when she finally started passing evaluations was stripping the screen down to roughly this stack. She could not talk herself into a counter-trend trade on the strength of a stochastic reading when the stochastic was not on the chart. Fewer tools meant fewer arguments to lose with herself, and fewer arguments lost with herself is most of what an evaluation actually rewards.

And here is the part that points past this chapter. If this stack feels insufficient, if you feel you need more tools to be confident, that is a psychological problem, not a tool problem. The cure is not more indicators. The cure is to get more familiar with the small stack, in many markets and many conditions, until you read what these three are telling you the way a fluent speaker reads a sentence. The sense of needing more comes from not yet trusting what you have, and trust comes from repetition. But notice what we just did. We diagnosed a charting question, and the answer turned out to be about you, not the chart. That keeps happening. The deeper you go into this craft, the more the decisive variable becomes the person making the decision, which is the exact territory the next book, *Trade Calm*, is built to map. The clean chart is not just good practice. It is a small piece of the funded edge, the unglamorous kind that survives a drawdown because there was never a twelfth indicator there to argue you out of your own rules.

The next chapter leaves the single chart behind and goes to the part of trading that decides whether you survive long enough to get good at any of this. Not the risk of one trade; we settled that in Chapter 4. The risks that survive good single-trade discipline. The correlated positions that quietly turn five small bets into one large one. The portfolio heat that adds up while you are watching each trade in isolation. And the steady psychological work of not dying, which is a different thing from the math of not dying, and harder. We are going to deal with all three.

CHAPTER 8, KEY IDEAS

- **Indicators are mathematical transformations of price, not new information.** They re-express what is already in the chart. Some forms reveal useful patterns; most are noise.
- **Use a small number of indicators consistently.** Three or four is enough. Hunting endlessly for the magic combination is astrology, not engineering.
- **Moving averages** define trend direction and provide dynamic support and resistance. The 200-period used as a bias filter, only trades aligned with its direction, is one of the highest-value rules in trading.
- **The RSI is a momentum indicator, not a reversal indicator.** Naive overbought/oversold readings get traders killed in trends. The valuable signals are divergence and behavior at the 40 to 60 zone.
- **The MACD is the workhorse.** The histogram is the most underused component. Combined with the 200-MA as a trend filter, its signals are reliable.
- **Stochastic, Bollinger Bands, and volume tools** each do one thing well. The Stochastic is a faster RSI, the bands measure volatility and flag the squeeze, and the volume tools confirm whether volume supports price. Pick deliberately and do not stack redundant ones.
- **The ATR is the most useful single indicator** for a developing trader, because it provides the volatility yardstick that makes stops, targets, and position sizes quantitatively meaningful. It also tells the funded trader, before the first order, whether a contract's normal daily range even fits the account's loss limit.
- **The honest professional stack:** 200-MA plus MACD plus ATR. Three tools, used with discipline, will outperform the trader running twenty. A clean chart is fewer arguments to lose with yourself, which is most of what an evaluation rewards.
- **Needing more tools is a psychology problem, not a tool problem.** The cure is repetition and trust in a small stack, which

is the first hint that the decisive variable is the trader, not the chart.

CHAPTER 9

The Religion of Not Dying

On a Monday morning some months into his trading, Marcus did everything right and lost more money than he ever had.

By now he had learned the lesson of Chapter 4. He honored his stops. He sized every position from his stop distance, one percent of the account, never more. That morning he placed seven trades, and every single one was a clean, disciplined, by-the-book trade. One percent long crude oil. One percent long natural gas. One percent long gasoline. One percent long heating oil. One percent long an oil-services equity future. One percent long the Canadian dollar, which tracks oil. One percent short the U.S. dollar, which moves inversely to oil. Seven trades, seven stops, seven careful position sizes. He believed energy was going higher, and he had expressed that belief seven different ways, and he felt, looking at his screen, like a professional running a diversified book.

He thought he had seven percent at risk, spread across seven bets.

He had seven percent at risk on one bet.

At 9:15, a headline crossed the wire: a surprise production agreement, and oil gapped down hard on the open. All seven positions moved against him at the same instant, because all seven were the same position wearing seven costumes. The Canadian dollar fell with oil. The dollar rallied, so his short lost too. Two of his stops slipped through thin pre-market liquidity and filled worse than the level he had set. By 9:20 he was down close to nine percent of his account, on a morning where he had broken not one rule from the chapter he thought was the whole game.

He called Sal, rattled, and said the thing every trader says the first time this happens. "I did everything right." Sal let it sit for a second. "You did everything right on each trade," he said. "You just made one trade seven times and called it seven trades. Chapter four keeps you from dying on a single trade, kid. This is the chapter about all the other ways to die."

Let me be clear about what this chapter is and is not, because the industry usually gets it backward. This is not the most important chapter in the book. That chapter was Chapter 4, the one about risk on a single trade, the survival rule, the stop-loss vow, the 1% sizing, the asymmetry of drawdowns. If you have not internalized that chapter, go back. Nothing here works without it.

This chapter is about the risks that survive Chapter 4. The deaths that find traders who have already learned not to die on any single trade. There are three of them, and each one has killed people far more sophisticated than Marcus or you or me. The correlated positions that quietly turn many small bets into one large one. The portfolio heat that accumulates while you watch each trade in isolation. And the slow psychological erosion of a long career, the steady work of staying alive across thousands of trades, which is a different and harder thing than the math of staying alive on one. We will take them in that order. And there is a fourth death this chapter has to add, one that did not exist in the same shape a generation ago: the funded account, where someone else's drawdown line decides when you have died, on a schedule you did not set. Dani has met that one five times. We will get to her.

A Brief Word on Sizing, Before We Go Past It

We are not going to re-derive position sizing here. You have the formula from Chapter 4: account times risk percent, divided by stop distance times dollar value per point, round down, every time. What I want to add is the deeper reason that formula is not negotiable, and a few sizing refinements that matter once you are running more than one position.

The deeper reason has a name. Risk of ruin. It has been studied formally for over a century, first in gambling theory, more recently in trading, and the conclusion is unambiguous and a little frightening. At any given win rate and reward-to-risk ratio, there is a maximum position size beyond which long-term ruin is mathematically certain, no matter how good the underlying strategy is. Cross that threshold, and you will eventually go broke. Stay below it and, assuming positive expectancy, you will eventually do well. The threshold is much smaller than retail traders intuit. The 1 to 2% rule you have heard throughout this book is not conservative paranoia. It is the mathematically defensible upper bound for the win rates and ratios that actual traders achieve. The point of Chapter 4 was survival. Risk of ruin is the proof that survival is a number, and the number is small.

Three refinements once you trade more than one contract. Fixed-fractional sizing, risking a fixed percentage recalculated for each trade, is the standard and your default. Volatility-adjusted sizing uses the ATR from Chapter 8 to set stop distances proportional to each contract's typical volatility. Hence, a volatile market gets a wider stop and fewer contracts, and a quiet market gets a tighter stop and more, keeping both dollar risk and relative risk constant. It is what most professionals actually use. And the Kelly criterion, the famous formula that calculates the theoretically optimal bet fraction given a known win rate and ratio, which you should know about mainly so you can leave it alone, because it assumes you know the true probabilities, which in trading you never do, and it is brutally sensitive to errors in those estimates, producing position sizes that would end your career. The 1 to 2% rule is essentially a very conservative fractional Kelly with the added virtue of being survivable when your probability estimates are wrong, which they always are. Save the Kelly math for after you have been profitable for two years.

Stop Craft, Past the Vow

Chapter 4 gave you the vow. The stop is placed before entry, never moved against you, and honored when hit. Chapter 3 gave you the order types. I am not going to re-litigate either. Use hard stops, bracketed with your target as a one-cancels-other order, on the overwhelming majority of trades, for the reasons you already know. What I want to add is the craft of managing a stop once a trade is working, because a stop is not only a death sentence you hope never executes. It is also a tool for taking risk off the table while a trade breathes.

The single most useful technique is the breakeven move. Once a trade moves a certain distance in your favor, typically when the unrealized profit equals your original risk, when you are "1R" up, you move the stop from its original level to your entry price. Now the trade carries zero risk. Worst case you scratch at breakeven, best case it runs, and you collect. This is powerful because it removes the specific psychological agony of watching a winner turn into a loser, and it lets you let winners run with no further capital exposed.

A more advanced version is the step trail. Once the trade is 2R in profit, move the stop to 1R, locking a small profit. Once 3R, move to 2R, and so on, the stop ratcheting up in steps, never giving back more than one R of accumulated gain. And the partner technique is scaling out. When a trade reaches 1R, close half the position; you lock a small profit and halve your exposure, and the remaining half can run to a much higher target, 3R or 4R, so that even if it eventually stops out, the whole trade is still modestly green. Scaling out significantly improves the emotional experience of trading and dampens the volatility of your equity curve without sacrificing much upside. Most professionals use some version of it. None of these violate the vow. The vow is that you never move a stop away from price. Every technique here moves it toward price, locking in survival as the trade earns it.

Risk-Reward, Without the Self-Deception

You already have the break-even table from Chapter 4. A 1 to 2 ratio needs about a 34% win rate to break even, 1 to 3 needs 25%, and the whole reason disciplined traders insist on a minimum ratio is that those numbers let you be wrong more often than right and still make money. I will not reprint the table. I want to warn you about the one way traders quietly cheat it.

The ratio can be gamed. A trader who wants to take a trade can manufacture a 1-to-3 ratio by setting an unrealistically distant target or an unrealistically tight stop. The number on the screen looks good, the trade gets taken, the fantasy target never prints, the too-tight stop gets clipped by ordinary noise, and the trader loses with the strange satisfaction of having "followed the rules." The defense is that both the stop and the target must be set by genuine technical levels, never by the desire to hit a target ratio. The stop goes at the premise-invalidation level, as in Chapter 4. The target goes at the next real obstacle, the next resistance for a long, the next support for a short. Then the ratio is calculated, not chosen. If the calculated ratio is below your minimum, you do not take the trade. You wait for setups where the natural stop and the natural target hand you the ratio you require. This will make you pass on most setups that look attractive at first glance, which feels like missing out and is in fact the entire point. The setups you skip because the math was not there are precisely the ones that would have bled your account. Patience for profitability. Always worth the trade.

Portfolio-Level Risk: The Trap That Got Marcus

Now the heart of the chapter, and the thing that actually happened on Marcus's Monday.

Everything to this point, his and yours, has treated risk one trade at a time. That is the necessary foundation. It is not sufficient. A trader can honor the 1% rule on every single position and still be carrying a catastrophic bet, because the positions are not independent. Marcus's seven energy-flavored trades were, functionally, one trade in oil sized at seven percent. He had diversified the costume and concentrated the bet.

This is correlation risk, and it is the silent killer of intermediate traders, the ones who have mastered single-trade discipline and have not yet learned portfolio discipline. It hits hardest exactly when you least expect it, during a shock, because in a shock correlations spike toward 1.0 and positions that looked diversified all move as one.

The legend here is not a retail trader in a spare bedroom. It is a hedge fund. In 2006, a fund called Amaranth Advisors, through one star natural-gas trader, built enormous, concentrated, correlated bets on the spread between natural gas contract months. On paper it was a book of many positions. In reality it was one gigantic wager on a single variable behaving a certain way. When natural gas moved against it, there was no diversification to cushion the blow, because there had never been any real diversification, only one bet in many shapes. The fund lost something on the order of six billion dollars in a matter of weeks and collapsed. The same disease that took nine percent of Marcus on a Monday morning took billions from professionals with risk committees and PhDs. The disease does not care about the size of the account. It cares only whether you understood how correlated your positions truly were.

The remedy is to think about risk at the portfolio level, not just the trade level. A few practical rules. Cap total portfolio risk: if you risk 1% per trade across five genuinely independent positions, that is 5% at risk if every stop hits, and the conventional cap for total open risk sits around 5 to 6%, but it must be adjusted for correlation, so five highly correlated positions should be treated as one or two for budgeting, which would have told Marcus his seven trades were really one or two and stopped him at the door. Cap exposure by theme: no more than, say, 2% of your account in aggregate energy risk regardless of how many energy setups tempt you, and the same for agriculture, currencies, metals, indices, which forces you to choose your best energy trade rather than stack all of them. Recognize correlation explicitly: some pairs are obvious, crude and gasoline, and some are real but less obvious, the dollar index and gold, the S&P and the Nasdaq, the Australian dollar and copper, so build a mental map of how the markets you trade move together and refuse to stack the correlated ones. And watch for the everything-goes-to-one environment: in true crises, 2008, March 2020, the depths of the European debt crisis, supposedly unrelated markets all become correlated as risk-off behavior dominates, and the diversification you were counting on evaporates exactly when you need it most.

That last point has its own legend, and it is the one every trader should keep in a back pocket. In 1998, a fund called Long-Term Capital Management, run partly by Nobel laureates, with risk models among the most sophisticated on Earth, was destroyed in weeks when a market shock drove correlations across its many "independent" positions toward one, all at once, in the direction it was not positioned for. The smartest risk model in the world did not save them, because the model assumed a diversification that the crisis erased. The defense, for them and for you, is the same and is almost insultingly simple. Reduce your overall exposure in periods of elevated systemic stress, regardless of how attractive your individual setups look.

One more portfolio rule, and it is the one that saves careers. Set a maximum daily and weekly loss limit, a number, say 3% in a single day or 6% in a single week, beyond which you stop trading and walk away from the screens. The purpose is to interrupt the destructive spiral in which a bad day triggers a revenge trade, which triggers a worse day, which triggers a worse revenge trade. In the language of the next book, that spiral is one of the named saboteurs, the Gambler, the part of you that believes a run of losses is owed a win and reaches for size to demand it back right now. You will not out-argue the Gambler in the moment, any more than you out-argued the Sunk-Coster in Chapter 4. So you bind him in advance with a number. When you hit the limit, you flatten everything, and you are done for the day, full stop. The discipline is brutal, and it has saved more trading careers than any indicator ever invented.

The Funded Account's Live Wire: Give-Back and Revenge

Everything above is how a trader manages risk on capital that belongs to him. Now change one thing, the only thing that has changed for the fastest-growing group of new traders in the market, and watch what it does. Make the capital somebody else's, and draw a line under it that you did not get to place.

A funded account, the kind Dani has bought five of and failed five of, comes with a trailing drawdown. The firm sets a maximum loss line, and on most modern accounts that line trails your highest equity of the day, or your highest equity ever, depending on the product. Make money, and the line rises behind you. Give some back, and on the most common structures the line does not fall with you. So a pullback into profit you had already banked on the screen does not feel like a smaller win. It reads, against that trailing line, exactly like a loss, because relative to the line it is one. This is the give-back trap, and it is the single most common way a capable trader fails an evaluation she was winning.

Dani failed her fourth evaluation on it without ever taking a bad trade. She was up nicely by mid-morning, the trailing line had ratcheted up behind her gains, and then the market did the ordinary thing markets do: it pulled back and chopped. Her open trades were fine. Her method was fine. But every tick of give-back was now eating into a cushion the firm's line had quietly redefined as her floor. The part of her that could not stand watching the number recede started trading to defend it, adding size, widening into trades she would never have taken on a calm Tuesday, until the give-back she was fighting became the breach she was trying to avoid. She did not lose because she was reckless. She lost because a line she did not set turned a normal pullback into an emergency, and she answered the emergency the way the Lizard always answers, by doing something.

The move is two-part. First, give-back tolerance, which you build by writing a give-back limit before the session, a number that says: when the day pulls back this far off its high, I am done, I protect the cushion as my own capital, and I walk. You decide it in the calm, you obey it in the heat, the same recursive handoff that runs all of risk management. Second, when two losses land in a row and the urge to force the third arrives, you run a two-loss circuit breaker, a hard stop and a cooldown, and you re-enter only an A-grade setup at base size. That is circuit-breaker discipline, and it is the funded-account version of the daily loss limit we just built, except the stakes are sharper because the firm is also keeping the count.

Dani learned both the expensive way. The give-back took her fourth evaluation, as we just saw. The revenge half showed up in her fifth, the same evaluation a profit target would later finish: early one morning, two quick losses inside the first hour, the certainty that the market owed her the next one, size up to collect the debt, and a third loss bigger than the first two combined, and the hole it dug was part of what the target then walked her out of by Friday. When she finally passed, her sixth attempt, she traded with a written give-back limit taped to the bottom of her monitor and a rule that two reds ended her morning, no exceptions, no negotiation with the version of her that wanted to argue. She passed the give-back trap and the revenge trap by refusing to let either one start: give-back tolerance and circuit-breaker discipline. Learn which of the two is more likely to end your next attempt, because for almost everyone it is one or the other. And for the rewiring that makes you able to obey a written number when every nerve says override it, the door is Trade Calm.

What I want you to see is that the funded account did not invent these failures. Marcus felt the same give-back agony watching his energy book bleed, and the same revenge pull on every red day of his life. The trailing drawdown just put a price tag and a referee on what every trader already does, which is why an evaluation is such a clean test. It does not measure whether you can find a trade. It measures whether you can sit still while a number you care about moves against you, which is the whole religion of not dying, billed by the firm and graded in real time.

Drawdowns: Managing the Bad Run

You already know from Chapter 4 that drawdowns are asymmetric, that a deep loss requires a far larger gain to recover, and that conservative sizing is the only real protection against the inevitable bad run. I will not reprint the asymmetry table. What I want to give you here is how to behave while you are inside a drawdown, because that is where the surviving trader and the dying one actually diverge, and it is not a sizing formula. It is a set of decisions made under emotional load.

Three rules. First, reduce position sizes during drawdowns. When your account is down 10% from its recent peak, cut your risk per trade from 1% to 0.5% temporarily. Smaller positions slow the bleeding while you work out whether this is normal variance or genuine strategy decay, and once you have stabilized, winning more than losing for a couple of weeks, you scale back up. Second, and harder, do not increase size after a winning streak. A run of winners convinces the brain the strategy is hot. It is time to press, and that is precisely the moment the strategy is least likely to keep working, because markets revert and edges decay and the trader fresh off a hot streak is statistically more likely to give it back than extend it. Size constant. Always. Third, have a maximum-drawdown shutdown rule. If the account drops, say, 20% from its all-time peak, you stop trading and go back to paper for a month while you reassess. The 20% mark is the signal that something has gone systematically wrong- the strategy, your execution, or a shift in the market that does not suit you, and the answer is to stop, diagnose, and restart only when you have found the problem. The shutdown is not punishment. It is the circuit breaker that keeps a bad month from becoming the end.

The Psychology of Not Dying

Here is the hardest part, and the part this book can introduce but not finish.

Every technical rule in this chapter only works if you can execute it in the heat of real trading, and the heat of real trading is precisely where rules go to die. You met the mechanism in Chapter 4. The reasonable version of you who sets the rules before the trade, and the unreasonable version who has to follow them during the trade, are not the same creature. The first one is calm and can do arithmetic. The second one has real money on the line and a nervous system that wants the bad feeling to stop. The whole architecture of risk management exists so that the first one can bind the second one in advance, where the second one cannot get loose.

So I am not going to re-explain that. I am going to name the moments where it bites at the portfolio level, because they are different from the single-trade moment. There is the moment you want to add an eighth correlated position because the theme is "really working," which is the Monday-morning trap dressed as conviction. There is the moment, deep in a drawdown, when cutting your size feels like surrender and pressing feels like courage, and they are exactly reversed. There is the moment the day pulls back off its high, and the give-back feels like an emergency that has to be answered now. There is the moment you hit your daily loss limit, or your two-loss circuit breaker, and every cell in your body argues for one more trade to "make it back," which is the Gambler asking for the keys. And underneath all of them is the oldest one, the one that has bankrupted everyone from Marcus to Amaranth to Dani's first four accounts: hope. Hope is the most expensive emotion in trading. Every time you let hope stand in for a rule, a stop, a size limit, a loss limit, a correlation cap, a give-back limit, you convert a controlled, survivable loss into an uncontrolled one.

The rules are not designed to make you feel comfortable. They are designed to take the decision out of your hands at the moment your judgment is most compromised. You set them before the trade because you are reasonable before the trade. You follow them during the trade because you are not reasonable during the trade. The reasonable past-you protects the unreasonable present-you, who then becomes the reasonable past-you for the next decision. That recursive handoff, repeated ten thousand times across a career, is the entire difference between the trader who is still here in a decade and the one who told his friends the markets were rigged. It is also, in miniature and on a clock, the entire difference between the trader who passes an evaluation and keeps the funding and the one who breaches it by Wednesday.

And this is the honest edge of what a field guide can do. I can give you the rules, the caps, the limits, the vow, the give-back number, the circuit breaker. I can show you Marcus on his Monday and Amaranth in its collapse and Dani under a trailing line and tell you they died of the same thing. What I cannot do, in a book about the market, is rebuild the part of you that knows the rule and reaches past it anyway, the part that feels hope as certainty and size as courage and a correlated stack as a diversified book and a normal pullback as an emergency. That rebuild is its own discipline, its own daily practice, its own book, and it is the one called *Trade Calm*. This book is teaching you to read the water and respect the current. That one teaches you to govern the swimmer. You will need both, and you will know, somewhere in your first real drawdown, or your first real evaluation, exactly why.

That, quietly, is the funded edge again, seen from the risk side. Not a setup and not a secret. The willingness to size small, cap the correlated stack, write the give-back limit, honor the circuit breaker, and sit still while a number you care about moves against you, repeated until it is just how you trade. It is what survives Marcus's Monday. It is what passes the evaluation. It is what holds the account after the first payout. Most people cannot do it, because their nervous systems will not let them. The whole of the work is becoming someone who does.

In the next chapter we go back to the market, into the layer beneath the chart that most traders never see, the order flow and microstructure that decides whether your good idea actually gets filled at a good price. The strategy that puts your edge to work comes after that. The risk framework you now hold, single-trade from Chapter 4 and portfolio-level from this one, is what keeps you in the game long enough for any edge to matter. Both together are the trader's craft.

CHAPTER 9, KEY IDEAS

- **This is not the most important chapter. Chapter 4 was.** This chapter covers the risks that survive single-trade discipline: correlation, portfolio heat, the funded account's trailing line, and the psychology of a whole career.
- **Risk of ruin is why the 1 to 2% rule is non-negotiable.** Past a certain size, long-term ruin is mathematically certain regardless of strategy quality. The threshold is smaller than traders intuit.
- **Sizing refinements for a multi-position book:** fixed-fractional as the default, volatility-adjusted (ATR-based) as the professional standard, and Kelly as the thing to know about and leave alone.
- **Stop craft past the vow:** the breakeven move (stop to entry at 1R), the step trail, and scaling out. All move the stop toward price, never away. They take risk off as the trade earns it.
- **Do not manufacture a risk-reward ratio.** Set the stop and target at genuine technical levels, then calculate the ratio. If it is below your minimum, skip the trade.
- **Correlation risk is the silent killer.** Multiple correlated positions are one big position. It got Marcus for 9% in five minutes and Amaranth for billions. Cap total open risk adjusted for correlation, cap exposure by theme, map your correlations, and cut exposure in systemic stress, when everything goes to 1, as LTCM learned.
- **Set a daily and weekly loss limit.** It binds the Gambler, the saboteur that turns a bad day into a revenge spiral. Hit the limit, flatten, walk away.
- **The funded account adds a trailing line you did not set, which weaponizes two failures.** The give-back trap turns a normal pullback into banked profit into a felt loss; the move is a written give-back limit that ends the day and defends the cushion as your own capital. The revenge trap turns two losses into a forced third; the move is a two-loss circuit breaker and cooldown, re-entering only an A-grade setup at base size. Their names: give-back tolerance and circuit-breaker discipline. It cost Dani two evaluations to learn them.

- **Behave correctly inside a drawdown:** cut size when down, never size up on a hot streak, and shut down to paper trading at a 20% drawdown to diagnose what broke.
- **Risk management is psychology dressed as math.** The reasonable past-you binds the unreasonable present-you in advance. Hope is the most expensive emotion in trading, and governing the part of you that feels it is the work of *Trade Calm*. Sitting still while a number you care about moves against you is the funded edge, seen from the risk side.

CHAPTER 10

The Tape and the Clock

Marcus learned the lesson of this chapter by getting chopped to pieces twice in one day.

In the morning he traded the first five minutes after the U.S. open, because that was when the chart moved the most, and he reasoned, sensibly enough, that the most movement meant the most opportunity. He was stopped out three times in eleven minutes by candles that lurched one way, then the other, then back, faster than he could think. In the early afternoon, bored during the quiet stretch after lunch, he took a clean-looking breakout at 12:40 and watched it die on the vine, drifting back through his entry on almost no volume, a breakout that nobody showed up to confirm.

Two losses, two different mistakes, one root cause. He had read the chart correctly both times and ignored the clock entirely. He sent Sal the two trades. Sal wrote back: "Right read, wrong hour. You keep walking into different fights without checking which fight you are in. The chart tells you what. It does not tell you when, or who is in the room. Learn the tape and the clock."

That is this chapter. Not the participants; you already met the five of them in Chapter 2: the hedger, the speculator, the arbitrageur, the market maker, and the algorithm under all of them. Not the order book itself; you met that in Chapter 3: the bids stacked below, the offers above, the spread between. This chapter is about reading those things live, in motion, and about the dimension the chart hides completely: time. When you trade, it turns out to matter nearly as much as what you trade, and almost no beginner knows it.

Reading the Footprints

You cannot see who is on the other side of your trade. But the participants from Chapter 2 leave footprints, and learning to read them is one of the more underrated skills in trading. The same price move can have a completely different meaning depending on who made it. A breakout driven by retail momentum chasing a headline looks identical on the chart to a breakout driven by an institution quietly accumulating a position. The first usually fades within hours. The second usually persists for days or weeks. The chart will not tell you which is which. The footprints sometimes will.

The order book, the depth of market you met in Chapter 3, is the first place to look, but now look at it as evidence of intent rather than just a queue. Three things repay attention. The depth at each level: is there a single contract bid at the current price, or are there five hundred? Because a thin book means a small order can shove the price, and a deep book means it takes real pressure to move it. The asymmetry between the two sides, when the offer side is much heavier than the bid side, sellers outnumber buyers in the immediate book, and the path of least resistance is down. And the walls, when a single level shows a vastly larger order than the levels around it- five thousand contracts bid where every other level holds fifty- usually an institutional limit order that acts as support or resistance while it absorbs the opposing flow. Remember the warning from Chapter 3, though. Walls can be spoofs, orders placed with no intent to execute, designed to fake demand or supply, and the tell is a wall that vanishes the instant price approaches it. Dani has a sticky note about that one.

The second footprint, the one Chapter 3 only gestured at, is order flow, the actual stream of trades hitting the book in real time. The time-and-sales feed, often just called "the tape," shows each trade as it executes, with size, price, and whether it hit the bid or lifted the ask. A continuous run of trades lifting the ask, in size, is aggressive buying pressure that has not yet shown up clearly on the price chart. A run of trades hitting the bid is aggressive selling. Reading the tape well takes years. But even the basic question, am I seeing more aggressive buying or more aggressive selling right now, adds a dimension the chart alone cannot give you. For most strategies, the tape is not your primary tool; it is fast and noisy and can mislead. For active intraday traders it is an essential second source. Even longer-horizon traders benefit from a glance before entering, to see whether they are about to trade into a wall or into thin air.

The Sessions: Why the Clock Beat Marcus

This is the part Marcus did not know existed. Futures trade nearly 24 hours a day, but the activity is nowhere near uniform. Volume, volatility, and the mix of participants change dramatically through the day, and the changes are predictable enough to trade around.

A typical U.S. futures day runs through phases. The overnight session, roughly 6 p.m. Eastern to 9:30 the next morning, is thin, with wider spreads, dominated by algorithms and a handful of overseas traders, where big news from Europe or Asia drives most of the real moves and, in their absence, prices drift in tight ranges. Overnight signals are simply less reliable, and many professionals do not trade meaningfully outside regular hours. The pre-market, roughly 7 to 9:30 a.m. Eastern, picks up as European desks trade U.S. markets and U.S. traders log in. The scheduled data- payroll, CPI, GDP- drops in this window and can produce instant 1 to 2% moves, choppier than the regular session because the book is thinner and price can lurch on relatively small orders.

The U.S. open, 9:30 a.m. Eastern, is the single most important moment of the day for U.S.-listed contracts. Volume spikes by an order of magnitude. The overnight imbalance, the gap between yesterday's 4 p.m. price and this morning's 9:30 price, gets resolved. The first thirty minutes are the most volatile of the day, offering the highest opportunity and the highest risk at once, and many disciplined traders avoid the first fifteen to thirty minutes entirely because the moves are large and the signal-to-noise is poor. This is the fight Marcus walked into in the morning. He brought a precise entry technique to the most chaotic fifteen minutes on the clock, and the chaos ate it three times.

Then the day settles. The mid-morning session, roughly 10 a.m. to noon, is when the market settles into its directional bias, patterns become more reliable, volume stays heavy, and the institutional algorithms that drive most of the day's flow are fully active. For many traders, this is prime time. Lunch, noon to about 1:30, sees volume drop sharply, markets consolidate in tight ranges, and patterns formed in this window tend to fail, which is exactly why Marcus's 12:40 breakout died; he traded a real-looking signal at the one hour of the day when real-looking signals are most often noise. The afternoon, 1:30 to 4 p.m., brings volume back and often establishes the day's most decisive move as institutional algorithms execute their daily quotas, and trends that emerge here often carry into the close. The close itself, the final thirty minutes, brings another volume spike as institutions rebalance and position for overnight, and the market-on-close order flow can produce sharp final moves that do not reflect the day's underlying direction, a classic source of head-fakes.

The point is not that you must trade every session. You should not, and most successful traders specialize in one window. The point is that the same chart pattern in two different sessions has very different reliability. A breakout at 10 a.m. on heavy volume is far more credible than the identical breakout at 12:30 on light volume. A trend-line break at the close on rebalancing flow can reverse entirely overnight. Knowing what session you are in, and how it behaves, is part of reading the chart in context. It is the clock that Marcus ignored, and it cost him both halves of that day.

There is a funded-account footnote to the clock, and Dani wrote it in losses. The most volatile fifteen minutes on the calendar are also the most efficient place to breach a trailing drawdown, because the open's noise can hit a stop through no fault of your read, and a firm's line does not grant a do-over for bad luck on a chaotic candle. One of her early evaluations nearly died in exactly that window, a clean setup shredded by open chop before the market had decided anything, half her cushion gone in minutes. She does not trade the first fifteen minutes of an evaluation anymore. She lets the open resolve, lets the mid-morning bias set, and trades the hour the professionals trade. The clock is not just an edge on entries. For a trader on someone else's line, it is risk management.

Spreads, Slippage, and the Real Cost of Trading

You already know the bid-ask spread from Chapter 3, the tax you pay on every trade, wider in thin contracts and thin hours. You know slippage, the extra cost when an order is large enough to walk through several levels of the book. I will not re-derive either. What Chapter 3 did not tell you is the third cost, and what all three add up to, because together they make a quiet but decisive argument about how often you should trade.

The third cost is fees. Exchange fees, regulatory fees, and broker commissions. Modern futures commissions at competitive brokers run roughly $0.85 to $3 per side per contract, with exchange and regulatory fees adding another dollar or two per side, so the total round-trip cost on a typical retail futures trade lands somewhere around $4 to $8 per contract. This is dramatically cheaper than a generation ago, when commissions were often $20 to $50 a side, but it still matters when you trade often.

Now add them up. Spread plus slippage plus fees is the combined drag, and it is what makes high-frequency strategies impractical for retail traders and even for many professionals. A scalping strategy that captures half a point of profit per trade, pays a quarter point in spread, and another five dollars in commissions per contract, is netting maybe seven dollars per contract per trade, and the math gets thin fast. The more frequently you trade, the more of your gross profit gets eaten before it reaches you. This is one of the strongest mathematical arguments for trading less, not more, and one of the reasons the most successful retail traders tend to be swing traders rather than scalpers. It is also, quietly, an argument the patient part of you and the impatient part of you will fight about constantly. The impatient part wants action and reads stillness as a missed opportunity. The arithmetic is on the side of stillness. Which side wins, in the moment, is a psychology question more than a math question, and you know by now which book that points to. It is also the same fight Dani had with the target in Chapter 7: the cost ledger simply keeping its own quiet count of every trade the impatience talked her into.

Market Cycles: The Rhythm You Can Sometimes Hear

We have covered trends and patterns. One more concept belongs here, because it interacts with the clock. Cycles. Markets often move through rhythms, recurring patterns of expansion and contraction, momentum and consolidation, with the dominant direction shifting at semi-predictable intervals. They come in several flavors.

Economic cycles drive the longest rhythms, the multi-year expansions and contractions that move the whole economy and drag markets with them, equities rising in expansions, bonds usually doing well in recessions, commodities following industrial demand. Most retail traders do not trade these directly. Still, every position is implicitly aligned or misaligned with the current phase, and going long equities in the early innings of a recession is fighting the cycle.

Seasonal cycles affect specific contracts predictably: natural gas firming from late August through January as winter demand approaches and weakening in spring as inventories rebuild, gasoline firming into the summer driving season and softening after Labor Day, agricultural contracts following planting and harvest, all real but with reliability that varies year to year, since a warm winter can break the gas pattern entirely.

Intraday cycles affect every contract within the day: the opening burst, the morning trend, the lunch lull, the afternoon move, the closing flush, the exact rhythm that beats Marcus, and awareness of them sets realistic expectations, since scalping the lunch lull is fighting the cycle and swing-trading the opening chop is fighting the chop.

And sentiment cycles are the most psychologically interesting, markets moving through optimism, euphoria, anxiety, and panic, each phase producing different behavior, every dip bought aggressively in euphoria and every rally sold in panic, with mean-reversion strategies thriving in normal regimes and getting destroyed in trends and panics, and trend-following thriving in euphoria and panic and getting whipsawed in normal regimes.

Cycles are probabilistic, not deterministic. They tilt the odds during certain periods; they do not guarantee outcomes. Traders who treat them as deterministic- it is October, so natural gas must rise, get burned. Traders who use them as one input among many, sizing up when cycles align with their other signals and down when they point the other way, extract real value.

The Microstructure Awareness Check

For each trade, get into the habit of a quick mental check across the factors in this chapter. It takes thirty seconds and meaningfully reduces the chance of being caught off guard, and it is precisely the check Marcus did not run on either of his two losing trades. What session are you in, a high-volume regime where signals are reliable or a low-volume one where they are noise? Who is dominating the flow right now, institutional accumulation, retail chasing, hedgers around a scheduled report? What does the order book look like, visible walls, or liquidity thin enough to whipsaw you? What is the spread, tight enough that your thesis survives it? What is on the economic calendar, any scheduled release that could blow through your stop in the next few hours? And what cycle phase are you in, with seasonal, intraday, and sentiment cycles aligned with your direction, neutral, or against it?

You do not need to write the answers down. The goal is awareness, not paperwork. Experienced traders run this check unconsciously in the seconds before they pull the trigger. Until that reflex develops, run it on purpose, and skip the trades that fail it. You will be skipping mostly the bad ones.

The next chapter takes everything we have built- the analysis, the patterns, the indicators, the two layers of the risk framework, and now the tape and the clock- and assembles it into actual strategies, the named, repeatable approaches working traders use to extract money from markets. Most strategies fall into a small number of families, and each suits different markets, temperaments, and time commitments. Choosing the right family is one of the most important decisions you will make. Let us get to it.

CHAPTER 10, KEY IDEAS

- **The chart tells you what. It does not tell you when, or who is in the room.** The participants are from Chapter 2 and the order book is from Chapter 3. This chapter is about reading them live, and about time.
- **Read the footprints.** Order-book depth, bid/offer asymmetry, and walls (real or spoofed) show immediate intent. The time-and-sales tape shows aggressive buying versus selling before it reaches the chart.

- **Time of day matters enormously.** Overnight is thin, the open is the most volatile and the noisiest, mid-morning is most reliable, lunch is noise, the afternoon often sets the decisive move, the close brings rebalancing head-fakes. The same pattern at different hours has very different reliability. Right read, wrong hour, is still a loss. On a funded account, the noisy open is also the easiest place to breach a trailing line, which is why Dani no longer trades the first fifteen minutes of an evaluation.
- **The real cost of trading is spread plus slippage plus fees.** Fees add a few dollars round-trip per contract on top of the Chapter 3 costs, and the combined drag is the strongest mathematical case for trading less, not more.
- **Cycles tilt probabilities.** Economic cycles drive multi-year direction, seasonal cycles affect specific contracts, intraday cycles shape every day, and sentiment cycles decide which strategy family is likely to work in the current regime.
- **Run the 30-second microstructure check before every trade:** session, dominant flow, order book, spread, calendar, cycle. It screens out a meaningful fraction of bad trades, including both of the ones that beat Marcus.

CHAPTER 11

The Strategies That Actually Work

By the time Marcus reached this point in his own education, he had a different system every week.

One week he was a breakout trader. The next, after three breakouts failed, he was a mean-reversion trader. The week after that, having read a thread about a man who got rich scalping, he was a scalper for four exhausting days. He was not building a method. He was channel-surfing, and his equity curve looked exactly like what it was, the record of a man who abandoned each approach at the first losing streak, right before it would have started working. He told Sal he was "still finding his edge." Sal asked him a question that stopped him cold. "You keep saying edge. Tell me what one is."

Marcus could not. Most traders cannot. So before we walk through the strategies, we are going to answer Sal's question, because it is the question the whole book has been circling, and because you cannot choose a strategy until you understand what a strategy is for.

What Is an Edge, Actually?

An edge is a small, repeatable reason that the math of your trading comes out positive over a large number of attempts. That is the whole definition. Not a secret. Not a setup. Not a feeling. A repeatable source of positive expectancy. Everything else in this chapter, every strategy family, is just a different machine for capturing one.

Recall expectancy from Chapter 4—probability of winning times average win, minus probability of losing times average loss. An edge is anything that makes that number reliably positive and keeps it positive across hundreds of trades. The word "reliably" is doing enormous work. Anyone can be positive over ten trades by luck. An edge is what is still there at trade number five hundred.

There are, in the end, only four places a real edge can come from. It helps to know all four, because it tells you immediately which ones are available to you and which are fantasies.

The first is an informational edge. You know something the market does not yet know, or you know it sooner. This is the edge of the hedge fund with the satellite-imagery contract counting cars in retail parking lots, and the edge of the desk with the fastest data feed. For a retail trader on a scheduled economic release, this edge is zero. You will never see the jobs number before the machines do. Cross informational edge off your list. It is not coming.

The second is an analytical edge. You have the same information as everyone else, but you interpret it better. This is real and partly available to you: the interpretive money we talked about in Chapter 2, the messy questions a human can sometimes answer better than an algorithm. But be honest about how crowded it is. Thousands of intelligent, well-resourced people are interpreting the same chart you are, and most of the obvious interpretations are already in the price. Your analytical edge, if you have one, will be thin and specific, a particular setup in a particular market that you have studied more deeply than the crowd. It is worth pursuing, and it is not where most retail money is made.

The third is a structural edge. You are positioned to collect a payment the structure of the market hands out. The market maker earns the spread. The trend-follower collects the premium paid by the crowd's tendency to under-react then over-extrapolate. The spread trader harvests a stable economic relationship. These are real, durable edges, and some of them are available to a disciplined retail trader who specializes.

The fourth is the one almost nobody talks about and the one that actually carries most surviving retail traders—a behavioral edge. Not knowing more or analyzing better, but doing the correct thing more consistently than the person on the other side of your trade. The market is full of impatient, hopeful, undisciplined traders who chase, who refuse to take stops, who size up after wins and revenge-trade after losses, who manufacture risk-reward ratios and abandon a sound method at the first cold streak, who are, in short, doing exactly what Marcus was doing all those weeks. When you stop doing those things, and they do not, the steady transfer of money from them to you is your edge. It does not require you to be smarter than anyone. It requires you to be more disciplined than the average participant, which, given who the average participant is, is an achievable and durable advantage.

Sit with which of those four is actually yours. Informational, no. Analytical, a little, thin and hard-won. Structural, yes, if you specialize. Behavioral, yes, and it is the largest one available to you, and it is almost entirely a matter of governing yourself. Which means the single biggest edge available to a retail trader is not on the chart at all. It is the difference between the trader you are at your calmest and the trader you become under pressure. That gap is the whole subject of the companion to this book, and now you can see why. *Trade Calm* is not a book about feelings. It is a book about protecting your largest edge from the only person who can destroy it: you. And it is, said plainly, the funded edge from the inside: the behavioral advantage is exactly what an evaluation is built to measure, and exactly what holds an account once you have one.

Two more things about edges, then we use the rest of the chapter to capture them. An edge decays. Every edge that gets discovered gets crowded, and crowding erodes it, which is why "the system that always worked" eventually stops, and why a working trader keeps adapting rather than worshipping one approach. And an edge is not a winning streak. This is the exact confusion Sal pointed at in Chapter 1, the cousin in Austin who had a great week and a story. A streak is what variance hands you. An edge is what is still there after variance is done with you. Marcus's problem was never that he lacked an edge. It was that he kept quitting each one during the variance, before the edge could show up. Choose a machine. Run it long enough for the math to speak. That is the whole discipline this chapter exists to start.

There Is No "The Strategy," Only Families

There is no single strategy. There are families of strategies, each suited to different markets, temperaments, time commitments, account sizes, and psychological constitutions. The trader's first big decision is not which indicator to use. It is which family to specialize in, and that is part intellectual: what kind of market behavior do I believe I can exploit, and part personal: what kind of trader am I actually capable of being.

What follows are the major families: trend following, mean reversion, breakout, scalping, swing trading, and spread trading. For each, I will give the underlying logic, the trader and market it suits, the strengths, the weaknesses, and the common failure modes. By the end, you should be able to narrow the field to the two or three that might fit you. One note first. Most of these, executed well, are positive expectancy. None works in every environment, on every contract, or without disciplined risk management. The strategy is the engine. The risk framework from Chapters 4 and 9 is the chassis. Neither alone is a vehicle.

Trend Following: The Strategy That Made the Turtles Famous

If you read one trading book that is not this one, make it something on the Turtle Traders. In 1983, a successful commodities trader named Richard Dennis bet his partner William Eckhardt that trading could be taught, that with the right rules and the right discipline ordinary people could become world-class traders. He recruited a group of complete beginners, the Turtles, trained them in a specific trend-following system, gave them millions to trade, and over the next several years they collectively made an enormous profit. The experiment proved Dennis right, and it proved something else this whole book leans on. The edge was in the rules and the discipline to follow them, not in the people.

The strategy was trend following, and its basic logic has barely changed in forty years because the truth it exploits has not changed. Financial markets, on most timeframes, spend more time trending than pure randomness would predict, driven by slow-moving fundamental information getting absorbed over time, herding, institutional flow that takes weeks to build, and the simple fact that humans extrapolate. The trend-follower identifies trends as they emerge, rides them while they persist, and exits when they break. In its purest form: define an entry that triggers as a new trend forms, the Turtles used a 20-day breakout, long on a new 20-day high, short on a new 20-day low; define an initial stop, the Turtles used a 2-ATR stop; size by volatility, risking a constant percentage per trade; trail the stop as the trend develops; and exit when the trailing stop fires, not when you feel the trend has ended and not at a profit target. The rules were a few pages. The complexity is all in the execution.

Two features make trend following psychologically brutal even when the rules are crystal clear. Most trades are losers, with a typical win rate around 35 to 40%; the majority stopped out for small losses, the strategy making money because the rare winners are enormous, often five or ten times the average loss. The math is beautiful over hundreds of trades. The experience is exhausting, since you spend most of your time being wrong, and most traders cannot tolerate a 60% loss rate even when they understand it, so they quit before the next big winner, exactly as Marcus quit. And you give back a lot of every winner, because a trailing-stop exit by definition only fires after the trend has reversed, so a move from $100 to $150 might exit at $135, leaving $15 "on the table," which feels terrible even though it is the unavoidable cost of catching the occasional $100 winner.

Trend following works best in markets that trend persistently- commodities, currencies, major indices- on longer timeframes, daily and weekly signals being far more reliable than hourly, and across diversified portfolios of many uncorrelated markets, accepting long strings of losers in each with the occasional big winner, the diversification smoothing the equity curve enough to make the whole thing psychologically survivable. If you are patient, can accept long losing streaks without losing discipline, and will commit to a multi-market portfolio, this may be your best fit. It is one of the most reliably profitable approaches in trading, has decades of out-of-sample evidence, and works part-time because daily-bar signals do not require staring at screens.

Mean Reversion: Betting on the Snap-Back

The opposite of trend following, it bets that prices return to an average after moving too far from it. Where trend following profits from the rare large move and accepts many small losses, mean reversion profits from many small wins and accepts the rare large loss when a trend overrides the signal. The basis is that markets in nontrending regimes, ranges, and consolidations oscillate, pushing up to where supply increases and falling back, pushing down to where demand increases and bouncing, and buying near the bottom and selling near the top of that rhythm extracts value. Simple version: identify a market in a clear range, mark its support and resistance, buy near support when an oscillator like RSI or Stochastic reaches oversold and turns, sell near resistance when it reaches overbought and turns, stop beyond the range boundary, target the opposite side.

Mean reversion generally carries high win rates; 60 to 70% is normal, modest risk-reward, usually 1 to 1 up to 1 to 2 because the range bounds the targets, and occasional catastrophic losses when the range breaks into a trend. The trader is positioned exactly wrong, and losses can be three to five times the typical gain. The strategy lives or dies on whether the stops are honored when the range fails. It works best in sideways, range-bound markets, on lower timeframes, in statistical pair trades, long one asset and short a correlated one when their spread widens, and at sentiment extremes when indicators like the VIX or put/call ratios reach historical limits. Its danger is that it explicitly trades against the trend, which feels comfortable, like buying low and selling high, and is mathematically lethal when the trend resumes. More mean-reversion traders die from a single failure to take a stop than from any other cause, which is to say, again, that the strategy is sound and the trader is the variable.

Breakout Trading: Riding the Energy Release

Breakout trading is a close cousin of trend following, both momentum strategies, but focused on the specific moment a range or pattern resolves into a directional move. Markets consolidate into well-defined ranges or patterns during indecision, then break out in one direction with energy, often on a volume surge and an immediate continuation. The approach: identify a contract in a defined consolidation, note the breakout level, place a stop-entry order just beyond it so the order triggers automatically on the break, place an immediate hard stop just inside the level once filled, and target the measured move of the pattern. Its appeal is clearly defined risk at the breakout level, asymmetric reward with measured-move targets often two to three times the risk, and mechanical execution that removes emotion from entry.

The drawback is the false breakout. A meaningful fraction of breakouts, perhaps 30 to 40%, fail: the price breaks the level, triggers entries, then reverses back through and stops out the new entrants, often running as far the other way as the breakout was supposed to run. False breakouts come from stop-running by larger players who target the breakout orders, momentum exhaustion at the level, and news arriving at inconvenient times. The defense is confirmation: a close beyond the level on a higher timeframe rather than an intraday poke, a volume surge, or waiting for a successful retest before entering, each layer reducing false signals at the cost of a later, smaller entry. The trade-off between speed and confirmation is personal. Breakout trading pairs especially well with trend following, since a breakout into a trend already in motion on a higher timeframe is a particularly high-quality setup.

Scalping: The Hardest Strategy in the Book

Scalping takes many small, quick profits from tiny moves, holding for seconds to minutes, dozens or hundreds of trades a day, sometimes capturing as little as one or two ticks. The mathematical appeal is the law of large numbers: a 60% win rate, risking two ticks to make two ticks across thirty trades a day, compounding into real money. The appeal collapses against reality. Transaction costs eat the profits, since each round trip pays the spread plus commissions, and on a two-tick gross profit you may keep close to nothing net, so scalping demands either a very high win rate or high average wins relative to costs, both hard to sustain. Execution must be near perfect, a few seconds of delay turning a winning scalp into a loser, requiring professional-grade platforms, low-latency feeds, hotkeys, and uninterrupted attention, so anyone scalping on a consumer app from a coffee shop will be slaughtered. The psychological intensity is brutal: hours of unbroken concentration where one bad trade can erase the day and trigger spiraling, and scalpers tend to burn out within a few years. And the skill curve is steep and expensive: most aspiring scalpers blow up before they get good, and the survivors often take a year or two of steady losses to reach breakeven.

If you are suited to high-intensity work, have professional equipment and connectivity, can commit several focused hours a day, and can survive the learning curve financially, scalping is a viable profession. For most retail traders, it is a road to ruin disguised as a fast path to riches. The education industry sells it aggressively because it is exciting and active. The math and the psychology mostly argue against it.

Swing Trading: The Sensible Default

If trend following is too patient and scalping too intense, swing trading, holding positions for days to weeks, is the middle ground that fits most retail lives. Swing traders work on daily and 4-hour charts, hold three to ten days, take a handful of setups a week, use a mix of trend and mean-reversion logic depending on the regime, spend thirty to sixty minutes a day on analysis plus a few minutes monitoring, and place trades mostly with bracket orders left to resolve automatically. The appeal is that it accommodates a normal life. You can swing trade while holding a full-time job or raising children. The time commitment is modest, the pressure moderate, and the strategies have decades of evidence behind them.

A typical approach: scan a watchlist of liquid contracts for daily-chart setups, pullbacks to support in uptrends, breakouts of consolidations, retests of broken levels; define entry, stop, and target for each high-quality setup with the standard pre-trade checklist; place bracket orders; check positions once or twice a day and let the brackets manage the trade; track results and refine. A disciplined swing trader generating 15 to 25% annual returns on a modest account is doing exceptionally well, statistically, since most professional money managers do not match that consistently. If you are starting with no strong reason to do otherwise, default to swing trading. Build the skill base, develop the discipline, learn what setups work for you, and only specialize into something more aggressive once you have years of profitable swing results behind you.

Spread Trading: The Relationship Trade

Last, and least familiar to retail traders, is spread trading, taking simultaneous long and short positions in related contracts to profit from the change in the relationship between them rather than the absolute direction of either. A simple example: a refiner profits from the difference between the price of crude it buys and the gasoline and heating oil it sells, the crack spread, so a trader can express a view on refining margins by being long a basket of refined products and short an equivalent quantity of crude, with no directional exposure to oil in the abstract, only to whether margins are widening or narrowing. Other classics: crush spreads, long soybean products and short soybeans on processing margins; calendar spreads, long the near month and short a distant one on changes in the term structure; and inter-market spreads, long the S&P and short the Nasdaq on rotation between value and growth.

Spread trading has real appeal. Reduced directional risk, since both legs move together to a degree, dampening broad market moves and leaving a position that can be roughly market-neutral on the underlying. Lower margin, because exchanges recognize the reduced risk. And more stable equity curves, since spreads move more slowly and predictably when the underlying economic relationship is stable. The downsides are lower potential returns, the reduced risk coming with reduced reward and none of the occasional multi-baggers of outright positions; harder analysis, since reading a spread requires understanding the underlying relationship and what moves it; and slower execution, since many platforms do not support native spread orders and force you to leg in one side at a time with the attendant risk.

Spread trading is the quietest corner of the strategy landscape, producing steady, unspectacular returns without the drama of directional trading, the preferred approach of many commercial hedgers and a meaningful slice of professional speculators, and it deserves more attention than retail education gives it. A note on the name, since this book is called *The Funded Edge*. Spreads are quiet, but quiet is not the edge in the title. The funded edge is not a strategy you select from a menu. It is the thing underneath all of these: the patience to run one sound machine long enough, the discipline to honor the rules through the variance, and the compounding that rewards both. It is the edge quiet enough to walk past on a shelf and durable enough to pass an evaluation and hold the account behind it. That edge is available in every family on this list, and we will name it plainly at the end of the book. For now, if you are inclined toward steady, low-drama returns and willing to learn the underlying economic relationships, spread trading is worth serious study.

Which Family Fits You?

Six families: trend following, mean reversion, breakout, scalping, swing trading, spread trading. Each genuinely viable. None universally superior. The question is which fits you, and the honest questions are mostly about your life and your wiring, not the market. Time: how many hours a day can you realistically commit? Scalping wants four to six focused hours, swing trading thirty to sixty minutes, trend following on daily bars fifteen to twenty, and you should match the strategy to the time you actually have, not the time you wish you had. Temperament: patient or impatient? Can you sit through long losing streaks? Trend following demands extraordinary patience; mean reversion offers more frequent wins; scalping feeds the desire for action and punishes any lapse of discipline. Capital: smaller accounts benefit from higher-frequency, faster-compounding approaches, and larger accounts can afford the patient drawdowns of diversified trend following. Skill-development cost: swing trading on daily charts has the gentlest learning curve, and scalping the steepest, with the highest beginner failure rate. And lifestyle, since a full-time job rules out scalping and a family probably does too, while flexible hours open more options.

Notice that almost every one of those questions is a question about you, not about the market. That is not an accident. The right strategy is the one you can actually execute with discipline over years, which means the binding constraint is rarely the strategy's logic and almost always your capacity to run it when it is cold. The right answer for most readers is some form of swing trading, possibly supplemented by trend following on longer timeframes for part of the account. Psychologically tolerable, financially viable, time-efficient, evidence-backed. It will not make you rich next year. With patience and discipline, it can build serious capital over a decade, which, if you have absorbed the chapter on what an edge actually is, you now understand is the only timescale on which an edge is real.

The Account Is a Choice Too: Dani and the Mismatch Trap

There is a second selection a funded trader has to make, and it is the one Dani got wrong for years without knowing it was a choice at all. Not which strategy. Which account.

Prop firms do not all draw their drawdown line the same way, and the difference is not a detail. Some accounts trail your loss limit intraday, tightening behind every tick of unrealized profit, so a trade that goes your way and then comes back can breach you on a number you never banked. Others trail only on the end-of-day balance, which leaves your intraday swings alone and only ratchets the line up after you have actually closed green. The industry has been moving toward the gentler end-of-day version, and several firms now let you choose the drawdown style outright when you buy the account. The rules change often, and they vary by firm and product, so confirm the current structure on the firm's own site before you pay for anything.

Here is why the choice is not cosmetic. An account whose drawdown style fights your temperament will end you on your own normal behavior, and you will blame yourself when the honest problem was a mismatch. This is the mismatch trap, and of the six traps it is the only one you solve before you place a single trade. Dani's weakest behavior, the one four failed evaluations had taught her, was give-back. She could not stand watching a cushion recede, and an intraday-trailing line turns every pullback into exactly that, a cushion receding against a line that will not give it back. For years she kept buying intraday-trailing accounts because they were the cheapest or the most advertised, and then failing them on the precise nerve they were built to press. The fix was almost insultingly simple once she saw it. She matched the account to her weakest behavior. She chose an end-of-day-drawdown account, which let her give back intraday without breaching, and on top of that she supplied her own daily loss limit, tighter than the firm's, because a couple of her accounts had no daily limit at all. An account with no floor is an invitation the Lizard will always accept. Same trader, same method, a different account, and suddenly the rules were working with her temperament instead of against it.

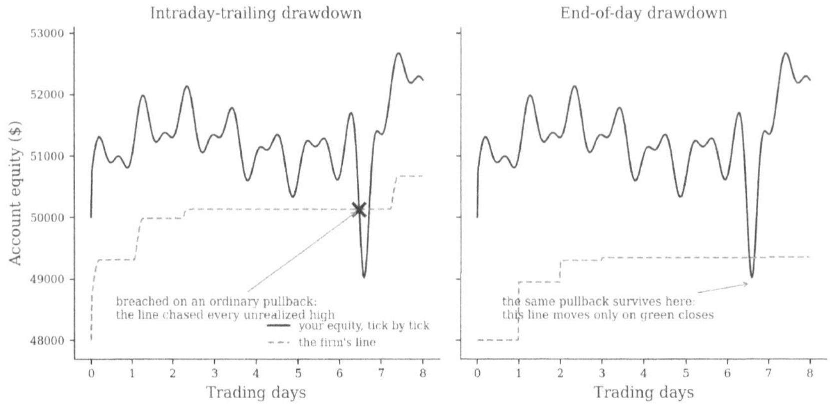

The same equity path under two rulebooks. The intraday-trailing line chases every unrealized high and ends the account on an ordinary pullback. The end-of-day line moves only on green closes, and the same pullback survives.

The lesson generalizes past prop trading. Whatever you trade, on whoever's money, match the structure to the trader you actually are, not the one you wish you were, and where the structure leaves a gap your weakest behavior would exploit, fill it with a rule of your own. Naming your weakest behavior honestly, before you pay, is the same thing as naming which drawdown style you most need to avoid. Do that work first, before any trade, because the account you cannot survive is the one mistake no amount of in-session discipline can fix.

In the next chapter we go into the advanced concepts that turn a competent intermediate trader into something more sophisticated: options on futures, volatility as an asset class in its own right, and what professional position management actually looks like.

CHAPTER 11, KEY IDEAS

- **An edge is a small, repeatable source of positive expectancy that survives hundreds of trades.** Not a secret, not a setup, not a feeling, and not a winning streak. A streak is what variance hands you. An edge is what is left after variance is done.
- **There are only four sources of edge:** informational (unavailable to retail), analytical (thin and crowded), structural (real,

if you specialize), and behavioral (doing the right thing more consistently than the other side). The behavioral edge is the largest one available to retail; it is governed entirely by you, and it is the funded edge from the inside, which is why it is the subject of *Trade Calm*.

- **Edges decay.** Crowding erodes every discovered edge, so a working trader adapts rather than worshipping one approach. Marcus's problem was never lacking an edge; it was quitting each one during the variance.
- **There is no single strategy, only families.** Trend following, mean reversion, breakout, scalping, swing trading, spread trading. Choosing the right family is one of a trader's most important decisions.
- **Trend following** wins 35 to 40% of the time with very large winners, works on diversified portfolios over weeks to months, and is psychologically brutal because of long losing streaks. The Turtles proved the edge is in the rules and the discipline, not the person.
- **Mean reversion** wins 60 to 70% with bounded targets, works in ranges, and lives or dies on honoring stops when the range breaks.
- **Breakout trading** captures the momentum release after a pattern resolves, with a 30 to 40% false-breakout rate that confirmation reduces at the cost of smaller targets.
- **Scalping** has the highest mathematical promise and the most brutal practical reality—professional infrastructure, intense focus, steep learning curve, unsuitable for most retail traders.
- **Swing trading** is the sensible default—moderate time, moderate pressure, evidence-backed, compatible with a normal life.
- **Spread trading** profits from the relationship between contracts, with reduced risk and steadier returns but smaller upside. It is quiet, but quiet is not the edge in the title. The funded edge is patience, discipline, and compounding, available in every family.
- **Match the strategy to your reality:** time, temperament, capital, lifestyle. Almost every selection question is about you, not the market, which tells you where the binding constraint really is.
- **For a funded trader, the account is a choice too.** Match the drawdown style to your weakest behavior, the mismatch trap, and the only one you solve before placing a trade. Dani kept

failing intraday-trailing accounts on give-back until she chose an end-of-day account and supplied her own daily loss limit. Verify each firm's current structure on its own site.

CHAPTER 12

The Advanced Toolkit

Two years in, Marcus was a different person. He had stopped blowing up. He had a strategy family, swing trading with a trend-following sleeve, and it ground out modest, unspectacular, compounding returns. And he was, for the first time, bored, and the boredom was making him reach.

He called Sal one evening wanting to talk about options, volatility, the things the professionals used, the dimensions of the market he sensed he was not yet engaging with. Sal listened, and then he said something Marcus did not expect. "The instinct is right. There is a second tier, and someday it is yours. But hear yourself. You are not reaching for these tools because your method stopped working. You are reaching because it started working, and working is quiet, and quiet is boring, and a part of you would rather have something complicated to do than let the simple thing compound. Notice that part. It is the same part that made you a strategy a week ago. We will learn the tools. But we learn them because they add edge, not because you are bored."

That is the right frame for this chapter, so that I will keep it. There is a genuine second tier of trading knowledge: options on futures, volatility as an asset class, position management at the portfolio level, and it opens up after the basics are in place. None of it is necessary for profitable trading. Plenty of successful traders never touch it. But for the trader who has the basics down and wants to expand, the second tier offers a real additional edge. This chapter is the introduction. I will not turn you into an options expert; entire good books exist for that, but I will give you enough to understand what is in the toolkit, when each instrument is useful, and how to integrate it into the framework you already have—the menu, not the cookbook.

Options on Futures: The Asymmetry Machine

An option is a contract giving the buyer the right, but not the obligation, to buy (a call) or sell (a put) an underlying asset at a specific strike price on or before a specific expiration date. The buyer pays a premium for this right. The seller, the writer, collects the premium and takes on the corresponding obligation. Options on futures are options whose underlying is a futures contract. They trade on the same exchanges, settle into the futures, and share the general structure of stock options, with some characteristics specific to the futures context.

The reason options exist at all is asymmetry. A long futures position has symmetric exposure: up X you gain X, down X you lose X, risk and reward equal and opposite. A long option has asymmetric exposure; a favorable move can produce a very large gain, an unfavorable move caps your loss at the premium you paid. The trade-off is that the premium is paid upfront; you have spent money to buy the asymmetry, and if the underlying does not move enough, the option expires worthless, and you lose all of it. The asymmetry can be sliced many ways. Buy a call to bet on a rise with downside capped at the premium. Buy a put to bet on a fall, same capped downside. Sell a call to bet the price does not rise, collecting premium with uncapped risk if wrong. Sell a put to bet the price does not fall, collecting premium with very large downside if it collapses. Or combine multiple options into spreads and structures for custom payoffs.

The premium comes from five factors, and once you internalize how each moves it, much of options trading falls into place. The underlying price: as the futures price moves toward the strike, the option gains value, and the sensitivity to the underlying is delta, around 0.50 at the money, approaching 1.00 deep in the money, near 0.00 deep out of the money. Time to expiration: longer-dated options are worth more because more time means more chance to move favorably, and the rate of value lost as time passes is theta, the buyer's enemy and the seller's friend, decaying not linearly but accelerating sharply in the final weeks, which is why short-dated options can collapse with frightening speed. Volatility: higher expected volatility means a more valuable option, the market's expectation being implied volatility, which tends to be high before scheduled events and to collapse after they resolve, the volatility crush, with sensitivity to it called vega, largest for at-the-money options with substantial time left. Strike price: strikes far from the current price are less likely to be reached and so cheaper; strikes close are dearer, and the structure of strikes against premiums forms the option chain. And interest rates have a small effect on long-dated options, negligible for typical retail trading. These are summarized in the Greeks: delta, gamma, theta, vega, rho, and professional options traders think largely in Greeks, often caring less about any single position's direction than about the aggregate Greek exposures of the whole portfolio.

For the trader just beginning to integrate options into a futures practice, three applications genuinely add value.

The first is protective puts, insurance for your futures positions. You are long, the trade is going well, your stop is in place, but a stop is an order, not a guarantee. In a fast move, especially around scheduled events or overnight, it can fill meaningfully worse than the level it triggered at, converting a planned 1% loss into 3 or 5% in seconds. A protective put eliminates that slippage risk. You buy a put on the same contract at a strike near or slightly below your stop, and if the underlying gaps down hard, the futures takes the loss but the put gains to offset it, capping your maximum loss at a known amount. The trade-off is the premium, which in quiet markets feels like wasted money, the protection never used, but in a year with one big surprise pays for many years of premiums. Use protective puts before scheduled events with high gap risk, around long weekends and holidays, when you have outsized profits in a position you want to keep but not risk giving back, and for overnight positions in gap-prone markets. Treat puts as you would any insurance, a small ongoing cost that absorbs catastrophic outcomes you could not otherwise survive, which, you will notice, is the same shape as the stop-loss vow from Chapter 4, bought with a premium instead of paid with a loss.

The second is covered calls, income from stagnant positions. You are long and well up; you have reached your target resistance, the market is consolidating below it, and you expect range-bound or modestly bullish action for several weeks. You do not want to close the position, but you do not expect dramatic near-term gains. So you sell a call on the same contract at a strike above your target, collecting the premium upfront, and if the underlying stays below the strike at expiration the call expires worthless and you keep both the premium and the position. In contrast, if it rallies above the strike, your futures keep gaining, but you are obligated to sell at the strike, capping your upside, partly offset by the premium. You have sold the right tail of your distribution for income, a great trade in most consolidating-or-mildly-bullish scenarios and a frustrating one in the rare case the underlying goes vertical, and the windfall passes you by. Covered calls work well as yield enhancement on positions you would otherwise hold, and many institutional managers use them systematically for a point or two of additional annual yield in exchange for slightly underperforming in strong rally years.

The third is directional bets with defined risk, the one most likely to appeal to active traders. You believe crude is going to rally hard over the next month. You could go long the futures, unlimited upside, downside at your stop, real-time risk requiring monitoring. Or you could buy a call: almost unlimited upside, maximum downside the premium paid, period, no stop to worry about, no gap risk, the worst case being that you lose what you paid. The call has defined risk; you know upfront that it cannot increase, leverage since a small premium controls a large notional, and no margin since the premium is the only capital at risk. The cost is time pressure: the option has an expiration, so theta decay works against you throughout the position's life, and a directional option trade requires not just a directional thesis but a timing thesis; the move has to happen within the option's lifespan, not just eventually. Use long calls or puts for high-conviction directional views around catalysts where you expect a sharp move in a known direction in a known window. Avoid them for slow, grinding trades with uncertain timing, which are better expressed in the underlying futures with a wider stop.

Once you understand basic calls and puts, you can combine them into a vast taxonomy of structures, vertical spreads, straddles, strangles, iron condors, butterflies, calendars, diagonals, ratios, each producing a specific payoff for a specific view. A few worth knowing as a starting point: vertical spreads, buying one option and selling another at a different strike same expiration, reduce cost and cap both sides at known levels, a cheaper way to express direction than a naked option; straddles and strangles, buying a call and a put on the same underlying, bet on a large move in either direction, useful around events where you expect volatility but not direction, and suffer from the volatility crush after; and iron condors, selling a put spread below and a call spread above, bet on the underlying staying in a range, a yield structure for low-volatility periods that carries large losses if the underlying breaks out. If you go deeper, Sheldon Natenberg's *Option Volatility and Pricing* is the standard reference and will take you considerably further than this book can.

Volatility as an Asset Class

Most traders think of volatility as a condition: the market is volatile, or it is not, rather than as a thing that can be traded. Professionals increasingly treat it as an asset class with its own dynamics. Implied volatility, the market's expectation of future volatility embedded in option prices, has predictable patterns. It mean-reverts, a spike during a crash drifting back down over weeks to months and a crush during complacency eventually spiking higher. It has term structure: the vol for options at 30, 60, 90 days usually rising with time, the shape of the curve carrying information. It has skew, index put options typically priced at higher implied vol than equidistant calls because the market prices crashes as more likely than booms. And it is negatively correlated with equity prices, the S&P and the VIX moving opposite directions a large majority of the time.

These open strategies target volatility rather than direction. Long volatility positions, long straddles, calls on the VIX, long-vol structures, profit when volatility rises and serve as portfolio hedges that pay off in crashes. Short volatility positions, covered calls, cash-secured puts, short straddles, short iron condors, profit when volatility declines or stays low, generating steady income in calm markets but facing catastrophic risk in spikes. The short-vol trade in particular has been quietly devastating across the last two decades. Every few years, a period of low volatility lulls a generation of short-vol traders into building large positions and treating the steady premium as a sustainable business. Then volatility spikes and the positions take losses far in excess of all the premium collected over the calm years. Selling volatility, as the old options-desk line goes, is like picking up nickels in front of a steamroller. The rhythm works fine right up until the steamroller is on top of you.

For the retail trader, approach volatility with caution. Long-vol positions as a portfolio hedge are reasonable. Short-vol positions are dangerous and require sophisticated risk management. Pure volatility products like VIX futures and options have peculiar mechanics, contango and roll yield, that catch many newcomers off guard. A simple, sensible approach is to use the VIX as a sentiment indicator rather than a tradeable asset. When the VIX is unusually low, complacency is high, and tail risk is elevated, it is a time to be cautious about leverage and to consider protective hedges. When it is unusually high, fear is extreme, and the market has usually already done much of its damage, often a buying opportunity for longer-horizon traders. The VIX as a tactical input to your decisions is more useful than the VIX as a direct trading target.

Portfolio-Level Position Management

Up to here we have mostly managed positions one at a time, which is the right starting point. But the professional thinks about positions in aggregate. A trade is part of a portfolio, and its value is its contribution to the portfolio's overall risk and return, not its standalone characteristics. A few concepts in the advanced toolkit. Correlation budgeting, building on Chapter 9, monitoring a correlation matrix across all open positions and refusing to stack highly correlated trades, with sophisticated versions using rolling correlations to detect regime shifts, the moments when previously uncorrelated assets begin moving together as a warning of systemic stress, the exact thing that turned Amaranth's many positions into one.

Greek aggregation, where if you use options your total exposure is not the sum of position notionals but the sum of your Greeks, total delta the directional risk, total gamma how that delta changes as the market moves, total vega the sensitivity to volatility, total theta the daily decay drag, and managing the portfolio means managing the aggregate Greeks, often adding trades specifically to neutralize unwanted exposures.

Capital allocation by strategy, where within one account you might run trend following in commodities, mean reversion in currencies, swing trading in indices, each with its own return, volatility, and drawdown profile, and sophisticated allocators rebalance capital between them by relative performance, regime, or systematic rule.

And drawdown management at the portfolio level, where once aggregate drawdown exceeds a threshold all positions get reduced, not just the losing ones, because the environment has likely shifted in a way that affects multiple strategies at once, the discipline being to scale down across the board rather than guess which strategy broke. These become important once you manage meaningful capital across multiple strategies. For a single-strategy trader on a small account, they are overkill. As the account grows and the strategies diversify, portfolio-level thinking starts to add real value, and eventually becomes the dominant level at which decisions are made.

When to Reach for the Advanced Tools, and When Not To

The risk of a chapter like this is that some readers close it convinced they should start using options and volatility products immediately. Most should not, and this is exactly what Sal was warning Marcus about. The advanced tools are only useful once the basics are in place and producing results. If you are not yet consistently profitable on plain futures, adding options or volatility products will not fix anything. It will add complexity you do not yet have the foundation to manage. The first job is to get the basic toolkit working. The second is to compound modest, steady results over years. Only the third, usually arriving after several years of consistent profitability, is to add the advanced tools.

A word for the funded trader, because it changes the timeline. Most proprietary-firm evaluations restrict you to the futures contract itself and do not permit options at all. A funded account often carries the same restriction, so for the trader chasing or holding firm capital, this entire chapter is mostly a tool for your own separate account, not for the evaluation in front of you. Confirm what your firm actually allows before you build any of it into your plan, because the rules vary by firm and product. There is a quiet mercy in that restriction. It forces the funded trader to make the plain instrument work first, which is exactly the order this book argues for anyway. Dani, long past the evaluation she finally passed, still trades nothing but the Micro and full E-mini on her funded account. Not because she could not learn the options chain; she could, but because the urge to reach for it shows up on precisely the quiet, working days when the simple thing is compounding, and she has met that urge before.

It is the same one that cost her the early accounts, wearing a more sophisticated costume.

When you are ready, add them one at a time. Do not try to add options trading, volatility hedging, and multi-strategy allocation all at once. Pick one, usually protective puts as portfolio hedges since they are the most universally useful, integrate it into your existing practice, trade it small for several months, build the intuition, and only then add the next. The trader who leapfrogs from basic competence directly into the advanced toolkit usually ends up with neither the basics nor the advanced material working well. The trader who masters each layer before adding the next builds a durable, compounding sophistication over time. The advanced tools are powerful, but power without foundation is just a more efficient way to lose money. And notice, one more time, the shape of the warning. The decision about whether to reach for these tools is not finally a question about the tools. It is a question about whether you can tell the difference between a real edge and a cure for boredom, which is a question about you. It always is, and it is the same question the funded edge turns on: the discipline to let the quiet, working thing keep working.

In the next chapter we turn to something less glamorous and more directly useful for most readers, the systematic practice of measuring your performance. This is the part that separates the people who actually improve over time from the people who only think they do. You cannot get better at what you do not measure. Let us measure.

CHAPTER 12, KEY IDEAS

- **The advanced toolkit is the second tier.** Useful but not necessary, for traders who have mastered the basics and want to expand. Reaching for it out of boredom rather than for edge is itself a warning sign.
- **Options on futures provide asymmetric exposure:** capped downside (the premium) and uncapped upside for long options, or the reverse for short. The asymmetry is the whole point.

- **Five factors drive option premiums:** underlying price, time, volatility, strike, interest rates, captured in the Greeks (delta, gamma, theta, vega, rho).
- **Three core applications for futures traders:** protective puts (insurance against gap risk), covered calls (yield from stagnant positions), and long calls or puts (defined-risk directional bets, especially around catalysts).
- **Volatility is itself an asset class** with mean-reverting, term-structured, skewed dynamics. Long-vol hedges crashes, short-vol generates income but carries catastrophic tail risk, like picking up nickels in front of a steamroller.
- **The VIX is most useful as a sentiment indicator,** not a tactical trade. Extreme lows signal complacency, extreme highs signal capitulation.
- **Portfolio-level thinking**, correlation budgeting, Greek aggregation, multi-strategy allocation, and portfolio drawdown management become essential as the account grows and strategies diversify.
- **Most prop evaluations and many funded accounts do not permit options at all.** For the funded trader, this chapter is mostly a tool for a separate personal account; verify your firm's instrument rules. The restriction quietly enforces the right order anyway; make the plain instrument work first.
- **Add advanced tools one at a time** after the basics produce consistent results. Leapfrogging usually leaves you with neither layer working, and the decision to reach is, again, a question about you, not the tools.

CHAPTER 13

The Numbers That Tell You the Truth

We need to talk about Cooper one more time.

You met him in Chapter 4, the technically gifted trader who could not take a small loss and blew up an account, the man running the same program that took down Barings. His shadow has hung over every risk rule since. Here is what happened after. Cooper did what most blown-up traders do. He took a break, licked his wounds, told himself he had learned his lesson, and came back with a smaller account and what he was sure were sharper instincts. He felt different. He felt like he had matured. He felt, deeply, that the trades he was now taking were better-quality trades made with better discipline.

What Cooper did not do was keep records. He did not log his trades. He did not calculate his win rate, his average win, his average loss, his profit factor, his expectancy, or any other quantitative measure of his performance. He had a vague sense that things were going better, that he was up, more or less, over the past few months, and that was enough.

A friend finally talked Cooper into a proper audit of his second-round trading. They sat down with twelve months of brokerage statements and built a spreadsheet from scratch: every trade, every entry, every exit, every fee. The numbers were shocking. Cooper's win rate, which he believed was around 60%, was actually 43%. His average winner, which he assumed dwarfed his average loser, was almost the same size, about 1.05 to 1. His total profit and loss after twelve months of "much-improved" trading was a small negative number. He had been losing money slowly while convinced he was winning.

Marcus, by this point in his story, did the opposite, and that is the whole difference between them. Marcus logged every trade, including the ugly ones, and once a month he sat down and let the numbers tell him things he did not want to hear. It was the least glamorous habit he had, and it was the one that compounded.

The disconnect between Cooper's belief about his performance and his actual performance is not unusual. It is the modal experience for retail traders who do not measure. Our memories of trades are biased. We remember the winners vividly, discount the losses, and mentally erase the trades we would rather not think about. The brain is not a reliable accounting system. The brain wants the story to be that you are getting better, and given any opening, it will edit the data to fit that story. The only defense is to measure. Systematically. Quantitatively. With the discipline of someone who knows the brain will lie to them if given any space at all.

This chapter is how to measure. It will not be glamorous, and it contains no dramatic payoff. It contains the single most consequential set of habits I can recommend, the habits that compound over years into the difference between the trader who actually improves and the one who only thinks he does—the difference, in short, between Marcus and Cooper.

The Trade Journal: The Foundation

A trade journal is a written record of every trade you take. Every one. No exceptions. It should capture the date and time of entry and exit, both timestamps down to the minute. The contract, specifically, MES, CL, ZC, including the month. Position size, how many contracts. Entry price, the exact fill, not the price you were aiming for. Stop-loss level, the level you committed to exit at. Target level, the price you committed to take profits. Exit price, the exact close. Reason for entry, a brief description of the setup, "50-day MA pullback in an established uptrend," "breakout above a 4-day consolidation on heavy volume," "bullish divergence at major support." Reason for exit: "stop loss hit," "target reached," "trailing stop triggered," or the important one, "closed early because I got nervous," because the point of the journal is not to document the trader you want to be, it is to document the trader you actually are. Outcome, profit or loss in dollars and in R-multiples: was it a 1R winner, a 0.5R loser? And notes: anything else worth recording, market conditions, emotional state, what you noticed, what you would do differently.

The journal can be a spreadsheet, a dedicated application, a notebook, anything that supports systematic entry and later analysis. Spreadsheets are fine and let you build whatever custom calculations you want. Several commercial applications, such as Tradervue and Edgewonk among others, automate some data collection by importing directly from your broker and add visualization on top. For most retail traders, a well-organized spreadsheet is sufficient, especially in the early years while you are still working out which metrics matter to you.

The discipline is simple to state and hard to keep. Every trade, logged, within 24 hours of the close. The trades you would rather forget are precisely the ones you most need to log. The trade where you broke your rules and got bailed out by luck must be in the journal. The trade where you froze and did not take the stop must be in the journal. The trade where you exited at the top by complete accident must be in the journal. The journal is a mirror, and if you only point it at your best angles it stops being useful. Cooper's real failure was not the 43% win rate. It was that for twelve months he never built the mirror.

The Metrics That Matter

Once you have even a few months of journal data, the metrics become calculable. Win rate, the percentage of profitable trades, is simple to calculate and easy to misinterpret, because a high win rate is not the same as profitability; a 70% win rate at 1 to 1 and a 50% win rate at 2 to 1 produce roughly the same expected return, so win rate only matters in the context of your reward-to-risk. Average winner and average loser, whose ratio is your realized reward-to-risk, which often differs from your planned reward-to-risk, and if your plan is 1 to 2 but your realized is 1 to 1.2, you are exiting winners too early, letting stops drift, or both, and that gap between planned and realized R is one of the most diagnostic numbers in trading. Profit factor, total dollars made on winners divided by total dollars lost on losers, 1.0 being breakeven and 1.5 meaning you made $1.50 for every $1.00 lost, with most profitable traders running between 1.2 and 2.0 and anything above 2.5 either extraordinary or a sign of insufficient sample size. Expectancy, the expected dollar or R outcome per trade, win rate times average win minus loss rate times average loss, positive meaning the strategy makes money over many trades and negative meaning no amount of position-sizing cleverness can save it, so the first question to ask of any approach is what its expectancy is and whether it is reliably positive.

Then maximum drawdown, the largest peak-to-trough decline in your equity, telling you the worst experience you have had with the strategy, important financially because you need enough capital to survive a drawdown of that size and psychologically because a drawdown meaningfully larger than your worst-ever tends to break even disciplined traders' execution. The Sharpe or Sortino ratio, a measure of return per unit of risk, the Sortino generally more meaningful for trading because upside volatility, big winners, does not actually feel like risk. The Calmar ratio, annualized return divided by maximum drawdown, return per unit of worst-case pain, is useful for comparing strategies with different risk profiles. And the number of trades, often overlooked and critical, because twenty trades is not a sample, two hundred is barely a sample, and two thousand starts to be informative, so the early-career trader concluding his "strategy" from 30 trades is reading tea leaves, the noise swamping the signal.

The Metric the Funded Trader Cannot Skip: Consistency and the Hero-Day Trap

There is one more number, and a funded trader has to track it whether she likes it or not, because a firm is tracking it for her. Call it the consistency metric: your single best day's profit as a share of your total profit. On your own account, nobody cares. Inside an evaluation, it can be the rule that fails you while you are up, and it is the home of one of the six traps, the hero-day trap.

Here is the mechanism, and Dani, our funded trader, walked into it early, well before she ever passed. Many firms impose a consistency rule, a cap on how much of your total profit any single day is allowed to represent, often somewhere around thirty to fifty percent depending on the firm and the plan. The logic is reasonable from the firm's side. They are trying to fund traders with a repeatable process, not a trader who hit one lucky lottery day and limped the rest. But the rule has a sharp edge for the undisciplined. Dani, on one early evaluation, had a green Thursday, a real one; the market handed her a clean trending day, and she pressed it, sized up because it was working, and booked a number that felt like the breakthrough she had been waiting for. It was, in fact, the breakthrough she had been waiting for, right up until she read the rule she had not read carefully, the one that said no single day could be more than a set fraction of her total. That one outsized day now made the rest of her required profit nearly unreachable inside the remaining limits. She had not lost a dollar. She had won too much on one day, and she spent the rest of that evaluation grinding small, deliberately capped days to claw the ratio back. It is a lesson she never needed twice.

That is the hero-day trap. The instinct it punishes is the most natural one in trading: press the day that is working, and on your own capital, pressing a genuinely good day is often correct. Under a consistency rule, it is a way to disqualify yourself while winning. The countermove is the one Dani now runs without thinking, and it lives in her metrics. She caps her profit on any single day at a fraction of her target, and when she hits the cap she is done, the same way she is done when she hits her loss limit, because the consistency line is just a loss limit pointed at her best self instead of her worst. She spreads the gains across days deliberately, treating a boring four-day climb to the target as superior to a one-day moonshot, because to the firm it is superior; it is the whole thing the firm is paying to see. And she watches the consistency metric in her monthly review now, her largest day as a percent of total, the same number the firm watches, so the firm never tells her something about her own trading that her own journal did not already know.

Call the discipline winning-day restraint. The hero day is the trap most likely to blindside the capable trader, because every other trap announces itself as a loss and this one arrives disguised as a win. Track the number. Cap the day. Spread the gains. It is the rare discipline that asks you to stop while you are ahead, which is exactly why so few can do it.

How to Actually Use the Metrics

The metrics are not just for evaluation. They are for diagnosis, and when something is off, they tell you where to look. Profitable on paper but losing in practice points to the gap between planned and realized R, most likely exiting winners too early or letting losers run past the planned stop, which is where edge gets bled away. Winning small and losing big, an average winner much smaller than the average loser, is the classic high-win-rate-poor-R pattern, taking quick profits but holding losers hoping they come back, and the remedy is psychological discipline around stops and around letting winners run. Long losing streaks, six, eight, ten in a row, could be normal variance, common in trend following, or a sign the strategy has stopped working in the current regime, and the way to tell is to read the streak against your historical streak distribution, a 10-loss streak being normal if it has happened before and alarming if your worst-ever was 5 and you just hit 12. High win rate with declining profit usually means the average winner has shrunk or the average loser has grown, a sign of drift, getting more conservative on exits and looser on stops over time. And outsized losses, a few trades 3x or 5x your normal loss, are nearly always stop violations or sizing errors, so watch the ratio of your largest loss to your average loss, and if it is more than 2x or 3x, you have a tail-risk problem.

The metrics are useless if you do not look at them. Reserve a recurring time to sit with the journal, compute the numbers, and ask what the data is telling you about how you are trading right now, what is working, what is drifting, what needs adjustment. This habit of periodic honest self-review is the practice that separates traders who improve from traders who plateau.

The Review Cycle: Weekly, Monthly, Quarterly

A useful structure uses three nested cycles. The weekly review, about thirty minutes every Friday, looks at the week's trades individually: were the entries triggered correctly, were the stops honored, were the exits according to plan, and notes any trade where you deviated and journals the why, emotion, fatigue, distraction, the pull to chase. Short and tactical, the goal being to catch small drifts before they become large ones. The monthly review, about ninety minutes the first weekend of the new month, computes the month's aggregate metrics, win rate, average R, profit factor, expectancy, drawdown, and for the funded trader the consistency metric, compares them to the prior month and the rolling three-month average, identifies trends, dissects any outsized winners or losers, and updates the trading plan if the data warrants. The quarterly review, about half a day at the start of each quarter, is a deeper structural look, all the quarter's trades sorted by setup type, which setups are working and which are not, and whether some markets are carrying all the gains. In contrast, others bleed, whether the strategy still suits the current regime, and whether structural changes are needed to the watchlist, the setup criteria, the sizing, or the hours of operation. The quarterly review is where strategic decisions get made.

Running these consistently, actually opening the journal, actually computing the numbers, actually thinking honestly about what they mean, is rare. Most retail traders, including profitable ones, do not do it. The ones who do compound their skill noticeably faster, because they have the data to identify what to work on. The ones who do not stay stuck at whatever level they happened to reach, unable to diagnose why their results will not improve. Cooper, in his second round, was working hard and going nowhere, and the reason was not effort. It was that he had no instrument pointed at himself.

Common Measurement Mistakes

A few warnings about how the metrics mislead: sample size, where twenty trades is not enough to conclude anything and two hundred is barely enough, so conclusions like "this strategy has a 75% win rate" drawn from small samples are almost always wrong because the variance dominates, and before changing your approach you should ask whether you have enough trades for a real signal. Survivorship bias, where journaling only the trades you remember well, the big winners and dramatic losers, distorts the picture, so the journal must include the unmemorable, boring trades or the metrics lie. Cherry-picking timeframes: the temptation to treat your best three-month stretch as representative, when the honest practice is to look over the longest available window including the bad stretches, because the best trader you have been is not who you are, and who you are is the average across all your stretches. Confusing process with outcome, since a single trade's result does not tell you whether the process was good, a bad trade can win by luck and a well-executed trade can lose because the market did not cooperate, so evaluate process quality, did I follow my plan, separately from outcome, did it make money, knowing that over many trades good process produces good outcomes and over a few they diverge wildly. And mistaking variance for skill or its absence, where a run of winners does not make you a genius and a run of losses does not mean you have lost your edge, both happening in well-functioning strategies. The temptation to tweak after a hot streak to capitalize or a cold streak to fix is one of the most destructive forces in retail trading. Stay consistent. Let the variance do its thing.

The Single Most Important Habit

If I had to compress the entire chapter into one sentence: journal every trade, calculate your metrics monthly, and look at the numbers honestly.

Most retail traders never do any of this. They carry vague impressions of their performance that are usually wildly disconnected from reality. They cannot diagnose their problems because they have no data. They cannot improve because they cannot see what is wrong. They blame the markets, the brokers, the algos, their luck. They never look in the mirror. The ones who actually improve do the boring, unglamorous work of measurement. They keep the journal. They compute the metrics. They look at the numbers honestly even when the numbers are uncomfortable. And they use the data to identify the specific thing to work on, not a vague aspiration like "trade better" but a concrete operational fix like "stop exiting winners early when the trade is up less than 1.5R" or "stop taking setups during the lunch hour because my win rate there is 30% lower than in the morning."

This is what professional development in trading actually looks like. Not glamorous. Not exciting. The only thing that reliably works. It is also, said one more way, the funded edge keeping its own books. The trader who measures honestly is building the exact evidence a firm is looking for, and more important, the exact evidence her own nervous system needs to trust the quiet process on the days it feels like nothing is happening.

But notice what the chapter keeps running into. The brain that edits the journal toward a flattering story. The discipline to log the trade you are ashamed of. The honesty to read a 43% win rate when you believed it was 60%. The restraint not to tweak the strategy after a hot streak, and the harder restraint to stop on a hero day while you are still ahead. Every one of those is a measurement skill that is really a psychological skill. The numbers are the easy part. Looking at them without flinching, and acting on them without ego, is the hard part, and it is not a spreadsheet problem. It is the same problem that has shadowed every chapter of this book: the gap between the trader you are when you are calm and the trader you become when it is your money and your story on the line.

That is where we go next, and where this book ends, because in the end it is the thing the whole craft rests on. We have circled the psychology of trading throughout. The next chapter faces it directly, and points you, finally and fully, toward the book that is devoted to nothing else. The market, it turns out, is mostly a mirror. What the trader sees in it is his own mind.

CHAPTER 13, KEY IDEAS

- **The brain is not a reliable accounting system.** It edits memory toward whatever story you want to believe. Cooper believed he ran a 60% win rate while actually running 43% and losing. The only defense is systematic, quantitative measurement.
- **The trade journal is the foundation.** Every trade, logged within 24 hours, including the ones you would rather forget. Without completeness, the metrics lie.
- **Core metrics:** win rate, average winner and loser, profit factor, expectancy, maximum drawdown, Sharpe or Sortino, Calmar, and number of trades. Each diagnoses a different aspect of the practice.
- **The funded trader tracks one more: consistency, the largest day as a share of total profit.** A firm's consistency rule (often roughly thirty to fifty percent, verify per firm) makes one outsized day a way to disqualify yourself while winning. That is the hero-day trap, and the discipline against it is winning-day restraint. The countermove: cap the day at a fraction of target, spread the gains across days, and watch the number the firm

watches. It is the rare discipline that asks you to stop while ahead.

- **Use metrics for diagnosis, not just evaluation.** Patterns point to specific problems: small winners and big losers mean exit discipline, declining performance means execution drift, outsized losses mean stop violations.
- **The review cycle:** weekly tactical (30 minutes), monthly aggregate (90 minutes), quarterly structural (half a day). Most traders skip all three. The ones who run them improve faster.
- **Sample size matters.** Twenty trades is noise, two thousand is signal. Do not change strategy on insufficient data.
- **Evaluate process and outcome separately.** Bad trades win by luck, good trades lose to randomness. Over many trades, good process produces good outcomes.
- **The single most important habit:** journal every trade, compute metrics monthly, look honestly at the numbers. The honesty is the hard part, and it is a psychological skill, not a spreadsheet one, which is exactly where the book turns next.

CHAPTER 14

The Inner Game

The market was doing nothing unusual. Marcus was the one coming apart.

It was the fourth red day in a row, a perfectly ordinary drawdown, the kind every sound strategy produces, and his own metrics said it was well within normal variance. He had done everything right. He had cut his size when the drawdown hit ten percent, exactly as Chapter 9 said. He had honored every stop. He had not revenge traded. On paper, on the spreadsheet he had learned to keep, he was a model of discipline.

And he was sitting at his desk at 10:40 on a Thursday with his cursor hovering over a setup that was not quite a setup, a trade that was not quite a trade, feeling a pull he could not name to click it, to do something, to make the losing stop. His heart rate was up. A voice in his head was building a reasonable-sounding case for why this marginal trade was actually fine, why the rules were too conservative, why a real trader would see the opportunity here. His finger was on the mouse. It was, he realized later, the exact posture of the man we opened Chapter 4 with, ten cents from his stop. Different decade of his trading life. Same finger. Same voice.

He did not click it. He closed the platform, walked away, and called Sal. He told him the whole thing, the four red days, the pull, the voice, the racing heart over a trade he knew he should not take. And he asked the question that the whole back half of his education had been building toward. "I know the rules. I know all of them cold. So why does it still feel like this? Why is it still this hard?"

Sal was quiet for a moment. Then he said: "Because you finally got to the real game. Everything before this, the charts, the contracts, the risk math, that was you learning the equipment. This, the thing you are feeling right now, the voice and the heart rate and the finger, this is the actual opponent. It was always the actual opponent. The market was never the thing you were fighting. You were."

We have been circling this for thirteen chapters. Every chapter in this book has, in one sense, been about psychology, through risk, through the gap between planned and realized execution, through the brain's habit of editing trade memories into a flattering story. But the inner game deserves its own chapter, because in the end, when all the technical work is done, and the rules are in place. The metrics are tracked, what remains is the trader alone at the screen, trying to do something his own mind is, in a thousand subtle ways, conspiring to undo.

There is a tradition in trading books of treating psychology as the capstone, the thing you study after you have mastered the technicals, the icing on the cake. That framing is wrong. Psychology is not the icing. It is the batter. It is what holds everything else together, what determines whether the technical knowledge you have accumulated can actually be expressed in real trades with real money on the line. The cliché that trading is 80% psychology has been repeated so often it has lost meaning, so let me make it concrete. The trader who has memorized every pattern and rule in this book and cannot execute under pressure will lose money. The trader with only a basic technical foundation who can execute calmly, mechanically, and consistently under pressure will make money. The difference is not the technical knowledge. It is the inner game.

I have to be honest with you about what this chapter can and cannot do, because honesty is the whole point of where it leads. I cannot, in one chapter, fix the patterns that hundreds of thousands of years of evolution and a few decades of your personal history have laid into your nervous system. What I can do is show you the opponent clearly. Name it, in its real parts, so you stop mistaking it for a charting problem. Give you the one tool a field guide can hand you. And then point you, plainly and without apology, toward the work that actually does the rebuilding, which is a different book and a different kind of effort than anything in these pages. Naming the opponent is the necessary first step. It is just not the last one.

The Three Brains at the Desk

Here is the most useful way I know to understand what happened to Marcus on that Thursday, and it is the model the companion to this book is built on, so I will introduce it here and let that book do the deep work.

You do not have one mind at the trading desk. You have three, layered on top of each other by evolution, and they do not want the same things.

The oldest is the Lizard. It is the ancient survival brain, fast, wordless, and concerned with exactly one thing: making the immediate bad feeling stop. The Lizard cannot read your trading plan. It cannot do arithmetic. When real money is on the line, and a loss is in front of you, the Lizard takes the wheel. Its entire program is to end the discomfort right now, which is why it will happily cancel a stop to make a paper loss disappear, never understanding that it has just traded a small certain pain for a large uncertain one.

The newest is the Professor. This is the slow, deliberate, rational mind, the one that read this book, ran the expectancy math, and decided, calmly, where the trade was wrong. The Professor writes the rules. The Professor is reasonable. The Professor is also slow, and easily shouted down, and rarely the one actually holding the mouse at 10:40 on a Thursday.

And between them is the Dog. The Dog is the emotional, social, habit-driven brain, the part that feels the racing heart, that wants to belong to the herd, that takes losses personally, that remembers the sting and flinches, that craves the dopamine of a booked win and the relief of a closed loser. The Dog is not stupid like the Lizard or wise like the Professor. The Dog is a creature of feeling and habit, and most of what you experience as the emotion of trading- the fear, the greed, the hope, the revenge- is the Dog reacting. The Lizard amplifying while the Professor watches, outvoted, from the back of the room.

Marcus's Thursday was a three-brain mutiny. The Professor knew the rules and agreed with them. The Dog felt the four red days as a personal wound and craved action to soothe it. The Lizard wanted the bad feeling gone now. Two against one, and the two that were winning could not read. This is not a character flaw in Marcus. It is the standard architecture of the human animal, and it is running, right now, in every participant in every market, which is both why the inner game is so hard and why mastering it is such a durable edge. Most of the people on the other side of your trades are being driven by their Dog and their Lizard. The trader who can keep the Professor in the chair, even some of the time, is harvesting the difference.

Why Your Brain Is Wrong About Markets

The three brains express themselves through a specific set of biases, and it is worth naming them, because you cannot watch for what you cannot name. These are not personal failings. They are universal features of human cognition, and the trader who thinks he is above them is just exhibiting one more of them.

Loss aversion, established by Kahneman and Tversky decades ago, means humans feel losses about twice as intensely as equivalent gains. Losing $100 hurts about twice as much as winning $100 feels good. It made sense for a hunter-gatherer, for whom a lost day's food was deadlier than a found one was helpful, and it is catastrophic in trading, where optimal behavior requires near-perfect symmetry about wins and losses. Loss aversion is the Dog refusing the stop because the loss hurts too much to accept, and exiting the winner too early because booking the gain feels too good to delay. The recency effect makes recent events feel more predictive than they are, so three winners feel like a hot streak that demands sizing up and three losers feel like a lost edge that demands shrinking, when three trades is meaningless variance. The result is that traders systematically size up right before reversion and down right before the return to normal. Pattern overfitting is the brain finding structure in noise, the savanna-scanning machinery inventing trends and reversals in what is mostly random, which is why most of the patterns the eye sees in short-term price are pareidolia, and only the ones confirmed across many contexts deserve action. Confirmation bias makes the brain weigh evidence for its existing hypothesis and discount evidence against, turning charts into Rorschach tests and keeping traders in losing trades long past the point the evidence should have ended them. The narrative fallacy makes the brain insist every move has a clean story, manufacturing an illusion of understanding that prevents the trader from accepting the irreducible uncertainty of the whole enterprise. And social proof makes the herd's behavior feel like evidence, which produces the bubbles and crashes, because by the time the consensus trade looks obvious, the move has already happened.

Notice that each of these is one of the three brains overriding the Professor. The point of naming them is not to defeat them by knowing them; you cannot, any more than knowing about an optical illusion makes you stop seeing it. The point is to recognize the feeling in the moment and decline to act on it, which requires a tool.

The One Tool a Field Guide Can Give You

There is exactly one technique I can hand you in a chapter, and it is the one every other chapter in this book has quietly been building toward. Protocol.

A protocol is a rule you write down when you are calm, the Professor in the chair, that you commit to following when you are not calm, the Dog and the Lizard at the wheel. The stop placed before entry is a protocol. The position size calculated from the stop is a protocol. The daily loss limit is a protocol. The pre-trade checklist is a protocol. Every one of them exists for the same reason: to take the decision out of your hands at the moment your judgment is most compromised. You set the rules before the trade because you are reasonable before the trade. You follow them during the trade because you are not reasonable during the trade. The reasonable past-you protects the unreasonable present-you, who becomes the reasonable past-you for the next decision.

This is why I have used religious language for the stop loss since Chapter 4. The discipline is not, in the end, a technique. It is a vow, taken by the Professor, that binds the Lizard. When the moment of weakness comes, and it will come on most trades, you hold to the vow because you took the vow, not because the situation in front of you feels right. The situation in front of you will almost always feel like it justifies breaking the vow. That is the Dog talking. The vow exists precisely because the situation always feels that way.

Protocol is what saved Marcus on Thursday. He did not out-argue the voice. Nobody out-argues the voice. He had a protocol, a written rule that marginal setups during a drawdown do not get taken, and a second protocol: when in doubt, step away from the screen, and he executed the protocols while still feeling everything, the racing heart, the pull, the reasonable-sounding case for the bad trade. That is the whole victory. Not the absence of the feeling. Action that holds steady while the feeling rages. It is also, in one sentence, the entire thing an evaluation is built to detect, and the entire thing the funded edge is made of.

The Door

And here is the honest limit of what I can do for you. I can give you the protocols. This entire book is, in a sense, a set of protocols. What I cannot do, in a field guide about the market, is the deeper work, the part that makes the protocols hold when the drawdown is not four days but four weeks, when the loss is not theoretical but a number that changes your life, when the Dog is not whimpering but howling. The Lizard has both hands on the wheel. I cannot, in these pages, teach you to recognize the specific saboteur that runs you, the Sunk-Coster who cannot close a loser because of what is already in it, the Gambler who believes a run of losses is owed a win and reaches for size to demand it back, and the others. I cannot teach you to feel the Lizard take the wheel and calmly take it back. I cannot rebuild your relationship with loss, with uncertainty, with your own nervous system under fire. That is not a chapter. It is a practice, daily and never finished, and it has its own book.

That book is called *Trade Calm*, and I want to be plain about why it exists and why this chapter ends by sending you to it rather than pretending to replace it.

Everything in this field guide is the equipment. The charts, the contracts, the risk math, the strategies, the journal. Sal called it the equipment on the phone with Marcus, and he was right. A person can own the finest equipment on the street and lose, because a mind operates the equipment, and the mind, untrained, will reliably betray the equipment at the worst possible moment. This book makes you literate in the market and competent with the instrument. It can hand you the protocols and show you, by naming them, the three brains and the biases and the saboteurs you are up against. What it cannot do, and does not pretend to do, is the actual rebuilding of the operator. The work of putting the Professor reliably back in the chair. The work of governing the Lizard and retraining the Dog. The work of becoming the calm one in a market of panicking humans, which, as we established in the chapter on what an edge actually is, is the single largest and most durable edge available to a retail trader, and the deepest layer of the funded edge.

That work is the whole of *Trade Calm*. It is not a book about the market. It is a book about the person trading it, the daily practice that turns the protocols from rules you white-knuckle into a temperament you inhabit. If this book has done its job, you finish it able to trade futures with real competence and real honesty about the risks. And you finish it knowing, in your body and not just your head, exactly why competence is not enough, and exactly what the missing half is. The missing half is the inner game, and the inner game has its own book. Marcus, on that Thursday, had just discovered the door. Whether he walked through it is the rest of his story, and the rest of yours.

I will give you the rest of what a field guide honestly can. A few routines stabilize the inner game enough to make the protocols livable, and they are not exotic. A pre-market routine that prepares the nervous system rather than generating trade ideas. A pre-trade checklist run every time, the way a professional pilot never skips the pre-flight no matter how many flights logged. A daily debrief that closes the emotional loop on the session. At least one full day a week off the screens, because the brain needs recovery and the traders who grind seven days burn out within years. Daily physical exercise, which metabolizes the stress hormones that trading pumps out with no physical outlet, is the cheapest and most neglected mental-game tool there is. Real sleep, because decision quality collapses without it. And a life and an identity outside trading, so that a bad month at the screens does not shatter your sense of who you are. These help. They make the inner game survivable. They are the field-guide-level intervention, and they are real, and they are not the deep work. The deep work is the other book.

And one more honest note, because the brand of this whole project is honesty. For some traders, the inner game runs deeper than routines and protocols can reach, into chronic emotional dysregulation, compulsive behavior at the screen, patterns of self-sabotage with roots far outside of trading. There is no shame in that and no shame in getting help for it. The traders I have known with the longest careers were almost all, at some point, in some form of structured psychological work, coaching, therapy, peer accountability. Brett Steenbarger's writing is a good entry point into the performance-psychology side of this and translates well to trading. The lone trader figuring out everything alone is a romantic image. In practice, the people who thrive have asked for help more than once.

The inner game is, in the end, the whole game. Everything else in this book is a vehicle for it, an external structure that exists to support an internal discipline. Master the inner game and the external structure becomes powerful. Neglect it, and the external structure cannot save you. That is the truest sentence in this book, and it is also, not by accident, the reason there is a second book.

We have one more thing to do before the long view. For thirteen chapters, Dani has been failing and learning at the edge of this exact problem, and she is about to reach the thing she has been chasing the whole time: a funded account of her own. In the next chapter, we follow her through the test, and then through the part the firms do not advertise, and almost nobody survives cleanly the morning after you finally win. The evaluation was never the hard part. Keeping it is.

CHAPTER 14, KEY IDEAS

- **Psychology is not the icing. It is the batter.** Technical knowledge means nothing without the inner discipline to execute it under pressure. The market was never the opponent. You are.
- **You have three brains at the desk:** the Lizard (ancient, wordless, wants the bad feeling gone now), the Dog (emotional, social, habit-driven, feels the racing heart and takes losses personally), and the Professor (slow, rational, wrote the rules and is usually outvoted). Most of the people across from you are run by their Lizard and Dog. Keeping the Professor in the chair is the edge.

- **The biases are the three brains overriding the Professor:** loss aversion, recency, pattern overfitting, confirmation bias, the narrative fallacy, social proof. Naming them does not defeat them. It lets you decline to act on them.
- **The one tool a field guide can give you is protocol.** Rules written when calm and followed when not, so the reasonable past-you binds the unreasonable present-you. Protocol, not willpower, is what holds the line, and it is exactly what an evaluation is built to detect.
- **Routines make the protocols livable:** pre-market preparation, a pre-trade checklist, a daily debrief, a weekly off-screen day, daily exercise, real sleep, and an identity outside trading. Real help, not the deep work.
- **The deep work, the actual rebuilding of the operator, is its own book.** This field guide hands you the equipment, names the three brains and the saboteurs (the Sunk-Coster, the Gambler, and the rest), and gives you the protocols. Retraining the mind that runs them, so calm becomes a temperament rather than a daily fight, is the whole of *Trade Calm.* Competence is half. This chapter is where you find the door to the other half.

CHAPTER 15

The Funded Account

Dani passed.

After four failed evaluations, after the loss she sat in past her stop, the spoof, the impatient counter-trend cluster, and the give-back, after the fifth one died on a profit target that turned her into a trader she did not recognize, the sixth one was quiet. She traded less. She wrote her give-back limit on a sticky note and a two-loss circuit breaker beneath it; she capped her best day on purpose, and she let three separate sessions end without a single trade because the setups were not there. On a Tuesday that felt like nothing at all, the platform showed the target met, every rule intact, and a firm she had paid a few hundred dollars handed her the keys to an account many times the size of her own. She had done the thing the title of this book is about. She got funded.

That was supposed to be the end of the story. It was the start of the hard part.

Three weeks later she took her first payout, a real withdrawal of real money from a firm's account into her own bank, the first dollar she had ever earned from trading size that mattered. And the following Monday, with the funded balance reset toward its base and the target she had chased for a year suddenly gone, she nearly gave the whole account back in an afternoon, not on a bad chart. On a quiet voice that said, now that you have been paid, it is the firm's money, not yours. We will come back to that voice, because it is the last and least-discussed of the traps, and it is the one that ends more funded traders than all the others combined. First, the machine she walked into, because it is now how a large share of new futures traders reach their capital, and almost nobody explains honestly what it actually tests.

What a Funded Account Actually Is

Strip away the marketing, and a futures prop firm offers a simple trade. You pay a fee for an evaluation, a test account with rules. If you trade to those rules and reach a profit target without breaking any of them, the firm gives you a funded account, its capital, not yours, and you keep a share of the profits you make on it, often most of them. The firm makes money on evaluation fees and on a cut of the winners. You get access to size you could not otherwise afford, with your downside limited to the fees you paid rather than a blown savings account.

The industry behind this has grown enormous in just a few years, and the reason is the same reason Dani was drawn to it. Most retail traders are undercapitalized, and a funded account is a way to trade real size without risking real savings. That is a genuine and useful thing, and it has gotten more trader-friendly lately, with several firms moving to one-time evaluation fees instead of monthly subscriptions, faster and more automated payouts, and the gentler end-of-day trailing drawdown we met in the chapter on strategy becoming closer to the standard. It is also, statistically, a hard test that most people fail. Published pass rates run low, often in the single digits to the mid-teens, and only a small fraction of funded traders ever reach a meaningful payout. The rules and the numbers differ firm to firm and change constantly, so treat every figure here as a direction, not a quote, and confirm the current terms on the firm's own site before you pay for anything.

Now here is the part the marketing will not tell you, and the part that should make you sit up if you have read this far. The firms are not, mostly, testing whether you can find good trades. They are testing whether you can follow rules under pressure. Every constraint they impose is a behavioral tripwire, engineered to catch the exact failures this book has spent fourteen chapters naming. The trader who passes is rarely the one with the best setups. It is the one who can hold the line when holding the line feels unbearable. Which means the evaluation is not really a trading test. It is a discipline test wearing a trading test's clothes, and you already own the curriculum for it.

The Rules Are This Book, Imposed From Outside

Walk through the standard rules and watch them turn into chapters you have already read, and into the exact failures that cost Dani her first four accounts.

The profit target is the goal of the evaluation, the number you must reach to pass. It looks like the friendly part of the rulebook, and it is the first trap. With a target in front of them and days ticking by, traders force trades to hit the number, manufacturing setups that are not there, sizing up to finish today. This is the target trap, the one that ended Dani's fifth evaluation while the chart was fine. The target is an outcome, and the moment you trade for the outcome instead of the process, you start taking the marginal trades that fail you. The move is the one this book has prescribed from the start. Trade your normal process, target or not, and let the number be a byproduct. The traders who pass do not chase the target. They run their process, and the target arrives.

The daily loss limit is a hard cap on what you can lose in one session, and crossing it ends your day or your account. It is, almost word for word, the daily loss limit this book told you to set for yourself back in the chapter on portfolio risk. The only difference is that the firm enforces it instead of you. The trap is the revenge spiral, the loss that begets the larger recovery trade that begets the limit breach, and the defense is the one you already have—the two-loss circuit breaker. After two losing trades inside your plan, you stand down for a cooldown before the limit is ever in danger. The firm drew its line in the sand. Your job is to stop well short of it, on your own line, which you drew first.

The trailing drawdown is the rule that ends the most accounts, and it is pure loss aversion in a costume. The firm trails a maximum-loss line up behind your gains, and at many firms that line never moves back down once it has climbed. So when you are up, and the market gives some of it back, you are not just watching profit shrink; you are watching your survival line approach. This is the give-back, the exact feeling from Chapters 4 and 9, the one that made Cooper cancel his stop and made Marcus slide his at eleven forty-seven, and the one that took Dani's fourth account on a perfectly ordinary pullback. Banked profit retreating registers in the body as a loss at double intensity, and the trader forces a trade to claw it back and breaches the line. The defense is pre-commitment. A written give-back limit, set in the calm before the session, honored without override, the same vow as the stop loss, pointed at the same enemy. You do not protect the trailing line by gripping the mouse harder. You protect it by deciding, in advance, how much give-back you will allow, and stopping there every time. And, as we covered when Dani chose her firm, you match the drawdown style to your temperament before you ever pay, because the account whose line fights your weakest behavior will end you on your own normal trading.

The consistency rule is the cleverest trap of all, because it punishes your best instinct. Many firms cap how much of your total profit can come from a single day. Have one enormous day and the rest of your account looks lopsided, and a profitable, rule-abiding trader can fail for being too good on a Tuesday. The rule exists to make sure you are a steady operator and not a one-lucky-day gambler. The behavior it catches is the hero day, the hot hand pressing because the day is running, the pull toward the screenshot-worthy number, the one that nearly caught Dani on a green Thursday early on. The move is restraint on your best day, deliberately, which feels insane in the moment and is exactly the skill the firm is paying to find. Cap your daily profit at a fraction of the target. When you hit the cap, cut size or stop. Build the evaluation out of ordinary days. The trader who can throttle a winning day on purpose has the rarest discipline in this business, and the consistency rule is just a machine for detecting whether you have it.

The minimum trading days and the scaling plan round it out, and both reward the same thing. Showing up to a process rather than swinging for a fast finish. You already know the answer. No action is a valid plan, boredom is not a setup, and size comes from the rules, not from the urge to be done. None of this is new. It is the book, handed back to you as a contract you signed with a stranger.

One more pressure deserves its own name, because it lives on the calendar rather than in the rulebook. Call it the clock. A minimum-day rule stretches the evaluation out; the fee you already paid compresses it. Somewhere in the middle sits a trader who has done everything right for two weeks and starts trading to be done rather than to be right, taking Friday trades a Tuesday version of her would have skipped. The clock is a constraint, not a countdown. The process does not know what day it is, and no firm is timing you as hard as the part of you that wants the verdict. Let the calendar spend itself. It is the cheapest thing on the table.

The Part Nobody Teaches: Keeping It

Here is the rule that is not in any firm's rulebook, and the one that ends more good traders than all the others combined.

Passing is the easy part.

There is an identity shift hiding in that sentence, and it is the real threshold. The morning after you pass, the trader who spent months trying to get funded has to retire, on the spot, and hand the keys to a different person: the one who operates funded capital. The chaser needed a verdict. The operator needs a Tuesday. Same hands, same method, but they do not want the same things, and every rule in this chapter exists because most people keep letting the chaser trade the operator's account. Dani's sticky note is really a change of job title. The work was never to pass. The work was to become someone whose ordinary day passes evaluations as a byproduct, and then to let that person run the business.

The account most traders blow is the one they already won. This is what nearly happened to Dani that Monday after her first payout, and it is worth slowing down on, because it is the most under-served problem in the entire prop world. After the payout, the funded balance reset toward its base. Her risk tolerance did not reset with it. A quiet voice, the same Dog and Lizard from the inner-game chapter wearing a new disguise, told her the math was different now. She had already pulled real money out. Whatever happened next was the firm's money, house money, found money, not the savings she had bled for on the early evaluations. And so, without quite deciding to, she sized up. The careful operator who had passed by trading less became, for an afternoon, a looser one taking trades a notch bigger than the ones that had earned her the account, because the downside felt abstract in a way it never had before.

She gave back most of a week's profit in three hours. And then she did the thing the early Dani could not have done. She caught it. The give-back muscle she had built over five failed evaluations recognized the feeling, the cushion receding, the survival line approaching, and this time she stopped before the line instead of after it. She closed the platform, and that night she did the post-payout work almost nobody does. She wrote down what had happened in plain language: *I treated the account differently because I had been paid, and the account does not care that I had been paid.* And she fixed it with three rules, set in the calm, exactly as she had learned to fix everything else.

This is the house-money trap, the sixth and last of them, and its move is the simplest to state and among the hardest to hold. First, the same size and the same stops that passed the evaluation on every funded trade, no exceptions, because the trader who passed is the only trader who has earned the right to operate this account, and sizing up is firing her. Second, a fresh process goal the day you pass, written down to replace the profit target you just retired, because the target was scaffolding and without it most traders drift, and a trader with no structure is a trader trading on feel. Third, bank on a schedule, deliberate withdrawals at planned intervals, so the account is something you steward rather than a number you are tempted to gun. Dani put all three on the sticky note next to the give-back limit. The funded account stopped being a prize she had won and became a business she ran. She is, as of this writing, still funded, which is a different and rarer achievement than getting funded, and the whole reason this book carries the title it does.

That completes the set. The six traps, by name: the target trap, the give-back, the revenge trap, the mismatch, the hero day, and house money. Each one is a normal human instinct with a firm's rulebook pointed at it, and each has a countermove you now own. You cannot circuit-break an urge you have not named.

The deeper shift underneath the three rules is the one the inner-game chapter pointed at. You have to stop being the person trying to pass and become the person who operates funded capital. That is not a technique. It is an identity, and an identity does not change because you cleared a profit target. It changes through practice, daily and repeated, the kind this book has pointed toward since the chapter on the inner game and the kind the companion book is devoted to entirely.

What This Means for You

If you are going to trade a funded account, and a great many of you will, because it is how an undercapitalized trader with skill now reaches real size, understand what you are actually signing up for. Not a shortcut. A discipline test, administered by a firm that has studied, far more precisely than you have, the exact moments traders break. The rules are not your enemy. They are the disciplines this book already taught, enforced by someone who will not extend you the benefit of the doubt the way you extend it to yourself at eleven forty-seven. A trader who has genuinely absorbed the risk chapters of this book is more prepared for an evaluation than most people who attempt one, because the evaluation is, in the end, a test of risk discipline under pressure, and risk discipline under pressure is the spine of everything we have done.

Two honest cautions before we move on. First, this book does not endorse any particular firm, and you should approach the whole industry with the same skepticism you bring to the rest of the trading-education world, because the rules differ firm to firm and change often. The only authority on a firm's current rules is the firm itself. Read them, in full, before you pay for anything. Second, a funded account changes the size of your capital. It does not change the trader operating it. If the disciplines in this book are not yet reflexes, a larger account lets you make the same mistakes faster and for more money. Build the trader first. The capital is the easy part to find.

There is a clean path through all of this, and it is the one Dani eventually walked. Before you pay a firm to find out which rule you will break, find out for yourself. Sit down with your journal and score yourself, honestly, against the five behaviors this book has named: give-back tolerance, circuit-breaker discipline, winning-day restraint, patience under a target, and the account-choice honesty the mismatch trap demands, and name the one most likely to end your next evaluation. The sixth trap, house money, cannot be scored in advance; it only shows itself after you pass. In Dani's case, it was the give-back line, the same enemy as everyone in this book. Then walk the arc in order, choosing the right account, the give-back, the hero day, the circuit breaker, the target, and the morning-after fight to keep it. And the deepest layer, the rebuilding of the operator who breaks the line at eleven forty-seven no matter how well she knows the rule, is *Trade Calm*. This chapter can show you the machine. That is where you learn to walk through it.

In the final chapter, we step back from the funded account, from the evaluation, from the single trade entirely, and look at the whole arc, the long project of building a trading life that lasts decades rather than chasing a windfall that lasts a week. We started this book calling trading a thing that can end an account in ninety days. We end it by calling it a profession, and by naming, plainly, the funded edge the whole thing is titled for.

CHAPTER 15, KEY IDEAS

- **A funded account is rented capital with a rulebook.** You pay for an evaluation, trade to its rules, and if you pass, you trade the firm's money for a share of the profits. It is how a large share of undercapitalized traders now reach real size, and most who attempt it fail. Terms and figures vary by firm and change constantly; verify on the firm's own site.
- **The evaluation is a discipline test wearing a trading test's clothes.** The firms are not mostly testing whether you can find good trades. They are testing whether you can follow rules under pressure, and every rule is a tripwire for a failure this book already named.
- **The rules are in this book, imposed from outside.** The profit target is the target trap. The daily loss limit is your two-loss circuit breaker, enforced by someone else. The trailing drawdown is the give-back, beaten by a pre-committed limit and the right account choice. The consistency rule punishes the hero day, beaten by restraint on your best day. Dani met every one of them the expensive way before she met them the disciplined way.
- **The white space is keeping it, not passing it. This is the house-money trap.** Most accounts die after the first payout, when the balance resets but risk tolerance does not, and the structure of the target is gone. "It is the firm's money now" is the costume the Lizard wears. The move: the same size and stops that passed, a fresh written process goal to replace the retired target, and banking on a schedule. Dani nearly gave

back the account she had won, caught it, and is still funded, which is the rarer achievement.

- **A funded account changes your capital, not your character.** A larger account only lets an undisciplined trader lose faster. Build the trader first.
- **Know your weakest rule before a firm charges you to find it.** Your journal already holds the answer if you read it honestly against the five behaviors this chapter named. Rebuilding the operator who breaks the line under pressure is *Trade Calm*. This chapter shows the machine; that is where you learn to walk through it.

CHAPTER 16

The Long Game

A few years after the Thursday in the inner-game chapter, Marcus got a message from a stranger.

It was a kid, twenty-something, who had found something Marcus had written online, and the message was almost word for word the one Marcus had sent Sal in his first week, the one about the eleven dollars that vanished into the plumbing. Where did the money go? Why is this so hard? Is there a trick? Marcus read it twice and felt the whole arc of his trading life fold over on itself, because he knew exactly what to say, and he knew that saying it would not be enough, because nobody had been able to say it to him either. It had to be lived. He wrote back two words to start, the same two Sal had once written him. "The plumbing." And then he did the thing Sal had done for him, which was to stay on the line for the years it would take.

Sal, by then, had mostly stepped back from the screens. His knees had won. He traded small, walked the dog, and answered the phone when Marcus called, which was less often now, because Marcus had become the kind of trader who did not need to call as much. Dani called him too, sometimes, though she had her own people now, the newer funded traders who found her the way she had found Sal, and asked her how she had passed, and got the same unwelcome answer everyone gets, that the passing was never the hard part. She was still funded. She had been for a while. The lineage that ran from the pits through Sal to Marcus and Dani and on to a stranger with eleven lost dollars is the oldest thing in this book, older than the electronic market, older than the contracts, and it is the thing Richard Dennis proved with the Turtles. It can be taught. Not quickly, and not to everyone, but it can be taught, by someone who learned it, to someone willing to do the years. This chapter is about those years.

I have had a particular conversation many times with people thinking about taking up trading. It starts with a question: what do I need to know to get started, and then forks. If the person wants to make money this year, this quarter, this month, I tell them trading is the wrong business for that goal, that there are faster ways with better odds, build a business, take a high-paying job. That trading as a quick-income strategy has roughly the expected outcome of the lottery with considerably more stress and self-recrimination. But if the person wants to build a practice, a long-term professional discipline that compounds over years into a real financial and personal accomplishment, then trading might be exactly right, and the conversation becomes very different and much longer. This final chapter is for the second person.

Trading as a Business

The first mental shift the developing trader has to make is to stop thinking of trading as a hobby, a hustle, or a gamble, and start thinking of it as a business. This sounds trivial. It is not. A hobby is unstructured; a business has processes. A hustle is opportunistic; a business is systematic. A gamble is hopeful, a business is calculated. A hobby is funded from your other income; a business is its own financial entity. A hobby has no accountability; a business has metrics, reviews, and continuous improvement.

When you treat trading as a business, certain practices become non-negotiable. You keep full records of every trade and every transaction. You separate trading capital from personal capital, in its own dedicated account. You build a written business plan covering your strategy, risk parameters, operating costs, performance targets, and contingencies. You operate on a schedule. You measure performance against targets. You review and adjust on a regular cycle. You invest in your own development. You handle taxes properly, treating trading income as the business income it is. And you set up the legal and structural foundations that protect you and optimize your tax position. None of it is glamorous. It is the unglamorous infrastructure of a real business, and it is what separates the trader who builds a durable career from the one who treats the account like a hobby and gets the predictable hobby results.

The business mindset also reframes losses, and this is where it connects back to everything in the inner-game chapter. In a hobby, a loss feels like personal failure. In a business, a loss is a cost of operations, an expected, budgeted, recurring expense the revenue model must absorb and still come out ahead. Restaurants pay rent every month whether or not the month is profitable. Traders take losing trades every month whether or not the month is profitable. The losses are not the failure mode. They are the cost structure. The failure mode is when the cost structure exceeds the revenue, which is what your monthly metrics tell you. The emotional weight retail traders attach to losses- I am bad, I lost money- has no equivalent in any other business, and reframing a loss as a line on a P&L drains much of its charge. It will not drain all of it. The part that remains is the Dog and the Lizard, and that part is the other book's work. But the business frame does real, available good.

The Trading Business Plan

Every serious trading business needs a written plan, not a vague intention but a document, reviewed quarterly, updated as you learn. It should cover strategy, what family you run, what setups, what contracts, what timeframes, and the documented edge, the win rate, average R, and expectancy you expect, from backtesting or live record. Risk parameters: your maximum risk per trade, per day, per week, the loss levels at which you cut size, stop for the day, or stop and reassess the whole strategy. Operating budget: what it costs to run the operation per month, platform, data, software, education, equipment, accounting, and your breakeven in trading P&L. Performance targets: your annual return target and quarterly milestones and how you will measure success. Contingency planning: what happens in an unusually large drawdown, a regime shift that breaks your strategy, an extended break, and what your fallback income is during difficult periods. A growth plan: how the approach evolves as capital grows, planned before you reach each stage so the transition is deliberate rather than improvised. And an exit plan: the conditions under which you would stop, after how many losing quarters, at what total drawdown, or at what capital target, which exists to permit you to stop without it feeling like failure, and which should include succession planning if you have dependents. The plan is not static. The discipline is actually to write it, actually read it, actually update it.

Most retail traders skip it entirely and operate on improvisation, and improvisation produces in trading exactly what it produces in any business: inconsistent execution, unrecognized drift, and eventual failure.

The Capital Structure

A few practical notes on capital. Never trade money you cannot afford to lose- advice that is old, ubiquitous, and almost universally ignored, the standard being that your trading capital should be money that, if entirely lost, would not change your fundamental life circumstances, not rent money, not retirement money. Still, money deliberately set aside whose potential loss is contained and survivable. This is, by the way, one more reason the funded route has grown the way it has. For a trader with skill and little capital, an evaluation fee is a far smaller and more survivable amount to risk than a self-funded account, which is a legitimate appeal as long as you remember the fee is the cheap part and the discipline is the expensive part. Maintain emergency reserves outside the trading account, three to six months of living expenses in a separate place, because the trader with no cushion is forced into desperate actions during a drawdown, sizing up to win it back. The trader with a reserve can ride out the bad months calmly because the household does not depend on the account producing income right now. Diversify income, especially in the early years, because the trader with another income source can be patient with his own growth while the trader fully dependent on trading from year one is under constant pressure to produce monthly returns. That pressure corrupts the discipline that produces long-term success, so keep an outside income through the development phase and only go full-time after multiple years of demonstrated profitability with enough capital to support both the business and your life through one to two years of zero trading income. And scale gradually, increasing position size deliberately and incrementally, resisting the urge to double up after a good year, because doubling size doubles the dollar volatility, and many traders find a strategy they executed cleanly at one scale breaks down emotionally at a larger one when the dollar losses exceed what their nervous system can absorb. Increase by twenty or thirty percent at a time, trade the new size for several months, confirm your execution stays clean, then increase again. Slow growth compounds. Reckless scaling blows up.

Continuous Development

The market changes. Strategies that worked in one decade stop working in the next. Volatility regimes shift, new asset classes emerge, new technologies change the competitive landscape, and the trader who got comfortable with what worked fifteen years ago and never updated is largely extinct today. Continuous development is not optional. In practice, it means reading, a steady diet of durable literature on strategy, market history, behavioral finance, and traders' memoirs, not the daily noise of financial media which is mostly entertainment dressed as information, with a reasonable target of one substantive book a month. It means backtesting and experimentation, continually testing new ideas on historical data, where most ideas die cheaply before they can kill your account and the few survivors earn small live tests scaled down enough to contain the cost. It means peer engagement, since other working traders are an enormous resource and the strongest signal of a worthwhile community is members who openly discuss losses and mistakes, not just wins. It means mentorship, accepting the gift if you can find a more experienced trader willing to compress years of bumping into walls, and being a good mentee, prepared, honest with your data, and not defensive. It means periodic structured learning, a conference or a workshop with a verified practitioner, chosen carefully because the education industry is full of expensive seminars run by people whose only edge is selling seminars. And it means reflection, sitting alone with your own data and experience and thinking honestly about what is and is not working, which is the deepest learning of all.

The Ethical Dimension

A note most trading books skip. Trading happens in an ethical context, and the context matters more than the explicit rules suggest. The most obvious territory is legal: insider trading, market manipulation, spoofing, and front-running are illegal and prosecuted, so stay safely on the right side of the line, not at it, because the marginal edge from skating close to legality is not worth a career-ending enforcement action and is usually not even meaningfully profitable at retail scale. The less obvious territory is your influence on others. If you talk publicly about trading, in any context where your views reach other people, you have obligations to them. Do not promote strategies you do not use. Do not show cherry-picked results that misrepresent your full record. Do not take payment to recommend brokers without disclosing it. Do not sell courses to beginners on topics you have not mastered. The education industry has a low average ethical standard precisely because so many participants violate these norms, and the result is that beginners pay for instruction that actively harms them. So if you enter that world, set a higher standard, because the world genuinely needs the difference. And the deepest territory is internal: the honesty you keep with yourself, the constant temptation to construct flattering narratives, to remember wins and forget losses, to credit skill for the wins and luck for the losses, to skip the journal entries that would document the trades you would rather not face. The traders who become consistently profitable are almost without exception people who have built an unusual relationship with honesty about themselves. They face their mistakes squarely, keep records that allow no escape from the data, and tell themselves the truth even when it is uncomfortable. That honesty is the moral core of the discipline, and it is also, not by coincidence, the same honesty the inner game demands. Without it no technique can save you. With it, even mediocre technique becomes powerful.

A Career, Not a Sprint

The trader's career, at its best, develops over twenty or thirty or forty years, not months. The first year is orientation, learning the vocabulary, the mechanics, the basic concepts, making every classic mistake, probably losing money, writing the foundations of the plan. Years two and three are consolidation, finding the strategies and markets that fit you, breaking even or slightly better, stabilizing the plan, building the journaling habit, beginning to recognize your own psychological patterns, and this is where many quit because the returns do not yet justify the time, not seeing that the foundation is being built underneath the surface. Years four through six are establishment: the plan working, returns positive and meaningful, scaling gradually, the psychological work growing more sophisticated, and the moment you stop seeing yourself as someone trying to learn trading and start seeing yourself as someone who is a trader. Years seven through fifteen are mastery: the strategies mature, the psychology mostly stable though always needing maintenance, the capital compounded into something meaningful, and the depth of experience to navigate regime shifts and personal disruptions and the occasional deep drawdown without panic. Beyond fifteen years is the territory of the few, an understanding of markets and self that cannot be transmitted through books or courses, belonging to people who made the long commitment to the work rather than the short commitment to the returns.

The path is long, and most who attempt it do not finish. The ones who do tend to find the trading they built over decades is one of the more deeply satisfying things they have ever done, not because of the money. However, the money can be considerable, but because of the depth of competence and self-knowledge the work demanded and rewarded. Sal would tell you that. Marcus, now, would tell you that. Dani, funded and still funded, would tell you that the account was never the prize; the person who could hold it was. And so would the kid with the eleven lost dollars, in fifteen years, if he does the work.

The Funded Edge

We have arrived, finally, at the phrase on the cover, and I owe you a plain naming of it, because I promised one back in the chapter on strategy.

The funded edge is not a strategy. It is not a setup, a secret, an indicator, or a contract. You cannot buy it, and you cannot be handed it. It is the thing underneath everything in this book, and it has three parts, all of them quiet. The patience to run one sound method long enough for the math to speak, instead of abandoning each one during the variance the way a younger Marcus did. The discipline to honor the rules when every nerve says to break them, the vow from Chapter 4 held across ten thousand trades. And the compounding that rewards both, the slow miracle we watched turn a modest stake into real wealth, not through any spectacular month but through the simple refusal to die, repeated for years. Patience, discipline, compounding. That is the whole of it. It is available in every strategy family, on every contract, to anyone, which is exactly why almost nobody captures it, because it is quiet, and quiet is boring, and the human animal would rather have something loud and complicated to do than let the simple thing compound.

It is called the funded edge for a reason that goes past the cover. It is the only edge that actually gets a trader funded, because it is the only thing an evaluation is built to find. It is the only edge that keeps a trader funded, because it is the only thing that survives the morning after the first payout, when the target is gone, and the Lizard calls the balance house money. Dani has it now. She did not have it through five failed evaluations, and the difference between the trader who failed them and the trader who holds a funded account today is not a setup she learned. It is the quiet, repeated work becoming who she is. That is the whole movement of this book, and the whole promise of the title. The quiet, disciplined work is the funded edge.

And you will have noticed it is not really a market edge at all. It is a character edge. It lives in the gap between the trader you are when you are calm and the trader you become under fire, which is the gap this book has pointed at from the first chapter and the gap the companion book exists to close. *The Funded Edge* can teach you to read the water and respect the current. It can hand you the patience and the discipline as rules. Whether they become who you are, quiet and durable, under real pressure, with real money, across real years, is the work of *Trade Calm*, and it is the work of the rest of your trading life.

If you choose this path, I wish you well. The work is hard, the failures will be many, the early years will test your conviction. But on the other side of all that, past the blow-ups, past the doubts, past the long stretches of mediocre returns, there is something real. A craft. A practice. A way of engaging with markets that is also a way of engaging with yourself. People have built lives on this work for centuries, and the people who do it well are extending a tradition with far more depth and integrity than the surface noise of the modern trading-education industry would suggest.

Welcome to it. Take it seriously. Treat the money with respect. Treat the markets with humility. Treat yourself with the honesty the work requires. And then put in the years.

CHAPTER 16, KEY IDEAS

- **Treat trading as a business,** not a hobby, hustle, or gamble. The shift changes everything and reframes losses as a cost of operations rather than a personal failure.
- **Maintain a written business plan** covering strategy, risk parameters, operating budget, performance targets, contingencies, growth, and exit. Review quarterly. Update as you learn.
- **Capital structure matters:** never trade money you cannot afford to lose, keep separate emergency reserves, diversify income in the early years, and scale position sizes gradually. The funded route is one way an undercapitalized but disciplined trader reaches real size while risking only the fee.
- **Continuous development is mandatory:** regular reading, backtesting, peer communities, mentorship, structured learning, and honest reflection on your own data.
- **The ethical dimension matters:** stay safely away from legal lines, hold yourself above the industry default if you teach or influence others, and cultivate ruthless honesty with yourself, the same honesty the inner game demands.
- **The arc is long**—orientation, consolidation, establishment, mastery, and beyond fifteen years the territory of the few. Most who attempt it do not finish. It can be taught, as the Turtles proved, but only to those willing to do the years.
- **The funded edge is patience, discipline, and compounding.** Not a strategy but a character edge, available to anyone and captured by almost no one because it is quiet and quiet is boring. It is the only edge that gets a trader funded and the only one that keeps them funded. Reading the water is this book. Becoming the kind of person who holds the line is *Trade Calm*.

Afterword

I want to close with a few honest notes that do not quite fit anywhere else.

The first is about humility. Everything in this book is true to the best of my knowledge and the conventional wisdom of working traders, but the markets are larger than any single book and any single perspective. Treat what you have read as a starting framework, not a final answer. Keep reading widely. Keep listening to people who do this work for a living. Keep testing ideas against your own experience and your own data. The honest practitioner is always a student.

The second is about expectations. If you read this book and decided you want to take up trading, understand that you are signing up for a long, difficult, frequently painful undertaking. Most people who attempt it quit within two years. Most who do not quit never reach consistent profitability. The ones who do usually take five or more years to get there. None of this is a reason not to try. It is a reason to try seriously, with proper expectations, and with a financial and personal life that can absorb the years of development without being destroyed.

The third is about money. Money is not a substitute for meaning. The trader who pursues trading mainly to get rich often makes terrible decisions, because the wealth obsession distorts the relationship to risk and reward. The trader who pursues it because the work itself is genuinely interesting- the puzzle, the discipline, the self-knowledge it demands- tends to make better decisions and, paradoxically, often ends up making more money. Aim for the craft first. Let the money follow.

The fourth is about regulation. Trading happens inside a regulatory framework that exists for the protection of market participants, including you. Take it seriously. Read the disclosures your broker provides. The regulations are not obstacles. They are guardrails on a road that, without them, would have a much higher fatality rate. Respect them.

And finally, a note about the larger context. Markets exist, ultimately, to allocate capital across the real economy. Every contract you trade has, somewhere upstream, a real economic purpose: a farmer hedging a crop, a producer locking in costs, a pension fund managing duration. As speculators, we are guests in a system that is fundamentally about real economic activity. It tolerates us because we provide liquidity and price discovery. It does not need us individually. A bit of humility about our place in the larger machinery is healthy. We are not the main characters in the story of markets. We are participants in a much older, much larger, much more important enterprise, and we should conduct ourselves accordingly, with respect, with care, and with the awareness that our behavior has consequences beyond our own portfolio.

Trade well. Stay alive. Take it seriously. Take care of yourself and the people who depend on you. And remember, when the markets seem chaotic, and the noise seems overwhelming. Your account is going through the kind of stretch that makes you question the whole project, that thousands of people before you have walked exactly this path and come out the other side, and that the discipline that carries you through is built one trade, one journal entry, one quiet decision at a time.

That, in the end, is the funded edge. It is yours if you want it. It has always been yours. The only question is whether you are willing to do the work, over years, that it requires. I hope, sincerely, that you are.

Now close this book. Open your journal. Take the next trade according to your plan. And the one after that. And the one after that.

Welcome to the practice.

Appendix A: The Six Traps at a Glance

Each of the six traps is a normal human instinct with a firm's rulebook pointed at it, and you cannot circuit-break an urge you have not named. Here is the whole set in one place, with the chapters where each one lives. Field guides earn their keep by being reopened. Reopen this page before every evaluation, and again the day you pass one.

The target trap. Strikes during the evaluation. The instinct it punishes: chasing the profit target, because a mind sent looking for setups finds them, lowering its grade one tick at a time. The countermove: process is the goal. A hard cap on trades per day, a no-trade day honored as a valid plan, and a session judged by the rules kept, not the dollars booked. Chapters 7 and 15.

The give-back. Strikes whenever you are up, and sharpest under a trailing drawdown. The instinct it punishes: banked profit receding reads in the body as a loss at double intensity, and you trade to defend the cushion until an ordinary pullback becomes a breach. The countermove: a written give-back limit, set before the session, honored without override. Protect the cushion as your own capital and walk. Chapters 9 and 15.

The revenge trap. Strikes after consecutive losses. The instinct it punishes: the Gambler, the part of you that believes a run of losses is owed a win and sends size to collect the debt. The countermove: the two-loss circuit breaker. A hard stop and a cooldown after two reds, and re-entry only on an A-grade setup at base size. Chapters 9 and 15.

The mismatch trap. Strikes before the first trade, at the moment you buy the account. The instinct it punishes: buying an account whose drawdown style presses your weakest nerve, then failing on your own normal behavior. The countermove: name your weakest behavior honestly, match the drawdown style to it, intraday trailing versus end-of-day, and add your own daily loss limit where the firm has none. It is the only trap you solve before placing a trade—chapter 11.

The hero day. Strikes on your best day. The instinct it punishes: pressing a hot hand into a consistency-rule breach. It is the only trap that arrives disguised as a win—the countermove: winning-day restraint. Cap the day's profit at a fraction of the target, stop at the cap, and spread the gains across ordinary days. Chapters 13 and 15.

House money. Strikes after the first payout. The instinct it punishes: the balance resets, your risk tolerance does not, and the retired target leaves no structure, so the account starts to feel like the firm's money. The countermove: the same size and stops that passed, on every funded trade. A fresh written process goal the day you pass. Bank on a schedule. Chapter 15.

Appendix B: The Field Checklists

The nine-step trade walkthrough (Chapter 5).

1. Confirm the contract: month, settlement type, size, tick value.
2. Set the stop at the level where the idea is wrong, the premise-invalidation level.
3. Compute dollar risk per contract: stop distance in ticks times tick value.
4. Set the target at the next genuine obstacle, never to manufacture a ratio.
5. Check risk-reward against your minimum. Below it, skip the trade.
6. Size the position: 1% budget divided by per-contract risk. Round down.
7. Confirm margin leaves buffer for adverse intraday moves.
8. Place entry, stop, and target together as a bracket.
9. Walk away. The trade resolves at the stop or the target.

The 30-second microstructure check (Chapter 10).

- Session: a high-volume regime where signals are reliable, or thin hours where they lie?
- Dominant flow: institutional accumulation, retail chasing, or hedgers around a report?
- Order book: visible walls, or liquidity thin enough to whipsaw you?
- Spread: tight enough that the thesis survives the tax?
- Calendar: any scheduled release that could blow through the stop?
- Cycle phase: seasonal, intraday, and sentiment cycles aligned, neutral, or against?

The six pattern-quality questions (Chapter 7).

- Is it completing at a meaningful level?
- Is it confirmed on multiple timeframes?
- Does volume align, declining in formation and surging on breakout?
- Does it align with the higher-timeframe trend?
- Did it take real time to form?
- Are there conflicting signals on the calendar?

The five-behavior self-audit (Chapter 15), before paying for any evaluation.

Score yourself honestly, from your own journal, on give-back tolerance, circuit-breaker discipline, winning-day restraint, patience under a target, and account-choice honesty. Name the one most likely to end your next attempt, before a firm charges you to find out. The sixth trap, house money, cannot be scored in advance; it only shows itself after you pass.

The post-payout protocol (Chapter 15), the day you pass.

- The same size and the same stops that passed the evaluation, on every funded trade. No exceptions.
- A fresh written process goal to replace the retired profit target.
- Bank on a schedule: deliberate withdrawals at planned intervals. Steward the account; do not gun it.

Glossary

Definitions in this book's own vocabulary.

Ask (offer). The lowest price any seller is currently willing to accept. Buy at market, and this is the price you pay.

ATR (Average True Range). A moving average of each bar's true range; the market's volatility yardstick. Used to set stops (two times ATR is a common default), targets, and position sizes, and to check whether a contract's normal day even fits your loss limit.

Back month. Any listed contract month beyond the front month. Thinner volume, wider spreads. Specialists only.

Bid. The highest price any buyer is currently willing to pay. Sell at market, and this is the price you receive.

Bid-ask spread. The gap between bid and ask; the tax paid on every trade. Tightest in the most liquid contracts.

Bracket order. An entry placed together with its stop-loss and profit target so all three go in as one unit.

Breakeven move. Moving the stop to your entry price once a trade is up 1R, removing all remaining risk from the position.

Cash settlement. Contract expiry by final cash payment rather than delivery. All major index futures settle this way, which is the reason evaluations are traded on them.

Circuit breaker (two-loss). A self-imposed rule: after two losing trades, stand down for a cooldown, and re-enter only an A-grade setup at base size—the countermove to the revenge trap.

Clearinghouse. The exchange entity standing in the middle of every trade, guaranteeing both sides. The reason futures carry no counterparty risk against the stranger who filled you.

Consistency rule. A prop-firm cap on how much of total profit any single day may represent, commonly somewhere around thirty to fifty percent; verify per firm. The machine that detects winning-day restraint.

Correlation risk. Multiple positions that move as one. Seven energy-flavored trades at 1% each are one trade at 7%—the silent killer of intermediate traders.

Daily loss limit. A hard cap on one session's loss. The firm draws one; you draw a tighter one first.

Daily settlement (mark-to-market). The clearinghouse credits and debits every account to the closing price every day. Futures do not let losses pile up silently.

Doji. A candle whose open and close are essentially equal: buyers and sellers fought to a draw. Meaning depends entirely on location.

DOM (depth of market). The visible queue of resting orders at each price level. A rumor, not a receipt; the biggest walls are often spoofs.

Drawdown. The decline from an equity peak. Asymmetric: a 50% loss requires a 100% gain to recover.

Edge. A small, repeatable reason the math of your trading comes out positive over a large number of attempts. Four sources: informational, analytical, structural, behavioral. Not a winning streak.

Evaluation. A prop firm's paid test: reach a profit target under fixed rules without breaching a loss line—a discipline test wearing a trading test's clothes.

Expectancy. Win rate times average win, minus loss rate times average loss. The only number that finally matters.

First Notice Day. The first day a long in a physically delivered contract can be assigned delivery. Exit or roll at least a week before it.

Front month. The contract month carrying nearly all the volume. The one you trade.

Funded account. A firm's capital traded under its rules for a share of profits after passing an evaluation. Changes your capital, not your character.

Give-back. Watching banked profit recede, which the body reads as a loss at double intensity, and a trailing drawdown converts into a survival threat. Countered by a written give-back limit.

Hedger. A participant whose real business is exposed to the underlying price and who trades futures to remove that variance. The slow, deep current of the market.

Hero day. An outsized winning day that breaches a consistency rule, disqualifying a trader while winning.

House money. The post-payout illusion that the account's downside is now abstract. The trap that ends more funded traders than all the others combined.

Initial margin. The good-faith deposit (a performance bond, not a loan) required to open a futures position. Set by the exchange, resized with volatility.

Leverage. Controlling large notional value with a small posted margin. A 1% move in the underlying can move margin equity around 19%: the multiplier and the cliff.

Limit order. Fill me at this price or better. Guarantees price, not execution for entries and targets.

Liquidity. The ease of transacting size without moving price against yourself. The single most important property when choosing a contract.

Maintenance margin. The minimum equity to hold a position, typically around 90% of initial. Breach it, and the broker liquidates: the private-account cousin of the trailing drawdown.

Market maker—the always-quoting firm on the other side of your instant fill. Earns the spread, never directional, vanishes in a panic.

Market order. Fill me now at the best available price. Guarantees execution, not price. For escaping, not entering.

Micro contract. One-tenth the standard size (MES, MNQ, MCL, MGC). The on-ramp the whole funded movement runs on.

Notional value. The full dollar value a contract controls (for the ES, $50 times the index). What your leverage is actually leveraged against.

Order flow (the tape). The live stream of executed trades: whether aggression is lifting the ask or hitting the bid, before the chart shows it.

Position sizing. Budget first (1% of capital or less), stop distance second, divide, round down. The hidden skill that decides survival.

Profit factor. Gross dollars won divided by gross dollars lost. 1.0 is breakeven; most profitable traders run 1.2 to 2.0.

R-multiple. A result expressed in units of the initial risk. A 2R winner made twice what the stop risked—the honest currency of the journal.

Risk of ruin. The mathematically certain destruction that follows position sizes beyond a threshold, and the threshold is smaller than intuition suggests—the proof behind the 1% rule.

Risk-reward ratio. Dollars risked against dollars targeted, both set by genuine technical levels and then calculated, never manufactured to justify a trade.

Roll. Closing an expiring front-month position and reopening it in the next month during the transition window.

Scaling out. Closing part of a winner (half at 1R, say) to bank profit and let the remainder run. Smooths the equity curve and the nerves.

Slippage. The difference between the price you expected and the price you got. Worst in thin books and fast markets; how a controlled loss becomes an uncontrolled one.

Speculator. A participant with no underlying business exposure, paid (if disciplined) for absorbing the risk hedgers shed—your camp.

Spoofing. Large resting orders placed to fake a level and pulled before they can fill. Illegal, prosecuted, and still ambient. Trade what fills, not what is resting.

Stop-loss. The pre-placed order at the level where the idea is wrong. Placed before entry, never moved against you, honored when hit—a vow, not a guess.

Target trap. A profit target converting a selective trader into a setup manufacturer. Countered by making process, not the number, the goal.

Tick, tick value. The smallest allowed price increment and its dollar worth (for the ES, 0.25 points and $12.50). The currency of every risk calculation.

Trailing drawdown. A prop account's maximum-loss line that ratchets up behind your gains, intraday on some accounts and end-of-day on gentler ones, and rarely comes back down—loss aversion, weaponized.

Variation margin. The daily cash flow of mark-to-market settlement between winning and losing accounts.

Win rate—the percentage of trades that profit. Meaningless without the size of wins against losses: Trader B is wrong more often than Trader A and runs the better business.

Further Reading

Every book in this business stands on cleared ground, and it is only honest to name the people who cleared mine. The vocabulary of R-multiples and expectancy that runs through the journaling chapters was popularized by Van Tharp in *Trade Your Way to Financial Freedom*. The casino frame in the risk chapter has been taught in some form by a generation of trading psychologists, most famously Mark Douglas, whose *Trading in the Zone* and *The Disciplined Trader* remain the standard texts on thinking in probabilities. The habit of reading a higher timeframe for bias, a middle one for the setup, and a lower one for the trigger descends from Alexander Elder's triple-screen work in *Trading for a Living*. Jack Schwager's *Market Wizards* interviews are the best evidence anywhere that wildly different methods can share the one trait that matters, which is the thesis of this book wearing other people's stories. Edwin Lefevre's *Reminiscences of a Stock Operator* is a century old and remains the truest thing written about the inner game. Brett Steenbarger bridges trading and clinical psychology better than anyone working. And Sheldon Natenberg's *Option Volatility and Pricing*, cited in the advanced chapter, is the standard reference it claims to be. Read them. The quiet edge compounds across books too.

www.ingramcontent.com/pod-product-compliance
Lightning Source LLC
LaVergne TN
LVHW050815061126
851857LV00012B/814
* 9 7 9 8 2 3 5 9 5 3 9 4 9 *